Sir Christopher Wren:
the Design of St. Paul's Cathedral

Sir Christopher Wren:
the Design of St. Paul's Cathedral

Introduction and Catalogue by Kerry Downes

Trefoil Publications, London
The American Institute of Architects Press
in association with
Guildhall Library

Published by Trefoil Publications Ltd
7 Royal Parade, Dawes Road, London SW6 in association with the Guildhall Library
Guildhall, London EC2

First Published 1988
Reprinted 1990

British Library Cataloguing in Publication Data

Downes, Kerry
    Sir Christopher Wren: the Design of St.
    Paul's Cathedral
    1. St. Paul's Cathedral (London) 2. Wren,
    Sir Christopher, 1632-1723   3.London
    (England) ---- Buildings, structures, etc.
    I. Title
        726'.6'094212   NA5470.S5

  ISBN 0-86294-091-5

Distributed exclusively in the U.S.A. and Canada by The American Institute of Architects Press,
1735 New York Avenue, N.W. Washington D.C. 20006, U.S.A.
ISBN 0-913-962-90-2

Printed and bound in Great Britain by Courier International Ltd

TRVNCI QVONDAM AC NVMQVAM
VITREI
AD MEMORIAM

CONTENTS

PREFACE

The Wren drawings for St Paul's have been familiar to me for many years in reproduction, and in the 1950s I saw nearly all of them in the original while working on a catalogue of the drawings of Hawksmoor. The opportunity to study them again in the ideal conditions of the Guildhall Library after their deposit there by the Dean and Chapter was a welcome one, and the invitation to make a completely new catalogue of them was a challenge. It has been possible to remedy many of the errors and some other shortcomings of the old *Wren Society* lists, and also to re-number the drawings in a more meaningful order incorporating those acquired from the Bute Collection in 1951.

For a number of reasons the work has taken far longer than anyone anticipated, but delay was fruitful in a number of cases where answers came up to knotty questions. The interlude of the 1982 Wren exhibition at the Whitechapel Art Gallery was also of great benefit; a number of the drawings were shown there and unique opportunities for comparisons were available. Some other causes of delay have been mundane, although time has also seen the conception of the project grow from a single typescript to the scale of the present volume in which almost all the drawings are illustrated.

In fact the only subjects not illustrated are either those too faint to reproduce, exact duplicates, or drawings on the backs of sheets which have no bearing on the history of St Paul's.

My thanks are due most of all to Ralph Hyde, first for his invitation, secondly for his patience and enthusiasm, and thirdly to him and his staff for their invariably cheerful assistance in the study of a body of material that starts by being physically unwieldy.

Particular thanks are also due to the Dean and Chapter of St Paul's, to whom the drawings still belong, and to the Warden and Fellows of All Souls, Oxford, who have generously allowed a number of the most important drawings in their possession, relating to St Paul's, to be reproduced.

Heartfelt thanks are also due to Frank Atkinson, the Cathedral Librarian, who found a number of interesting items in library cupboards and kindly communicated them to me; to Terry Friedman for his advocacy; to Peter Carter and Dennis Mannina for discussion and illuminating insights; to Robert Crayford and Ben Weinreb for clues which otherwise I should have missed.

Kerry Downes
Department of History of Art
University of Reading

INTRODUCTION

Sir Christopher Wren

Sir Christopher Wren is the most famous of British architects, and one of the greatest. Whether he is unique in stature is a matter for debate, and one that becomes academic in the face of St. Paul's Cathedral, unquestionably one of the most remarkable buildings, not only in Great Britain, but in the world. The architect's son and first biographer thought it a sufficient achievement that his father had lived to see the completion of a building whose design had exercised his talents for forty-five years and whose construction had occupied thirty-five. The Great Fire of London of 1666 turned a new cathedral from a desirable ideal into a necessity; without St Paul's Wren would still have been a great architect, although more of his life's work might have gone into other areas of activity.

Wren was born on 20 October 1632, the second of three generations of Christophers, at East Knoyle, a small Wiltshire village where his father was Rector. The elder Christopher was a man of both considerable piety and great ingenuity in the pre-Baconian school. Among his inventions were a numerological prediction of a disaster in 1666, an artificial serpentine stream and a new form of roof construction which he applied to his rectory. The future architect grew up with the religious and political values of the established Church of England and the monarchy during a period when both were being questioned; he was a little over sixteen when Charles I was condemned to death for treason. But against this background of certainty under attack he questioned everything else. In 1649/50 he went up to Wadham College, Oxford, proceeding in 1653 to a fellowship of All Souls. In Oxford he met like-minded adherents of the new Baconian science (or "experimental philosophy") and became a leading member of the group, bridging both sides of the religious and political controversy, who would form the nucleus of the Royal Society in 1660, the year of Charles II's Restoration. In 1657 Wren had been appointed Professor of Astronomy at Gresham College in the City of London but when the college was closed a year later after the death of Oliver Cromwell, Dr Wren returned to Oxford, where in 1661 he was elected to a chair in astronomy.

If Wren had died at thirty he would be remembered as a brilliant young scientist, the "miracle of a youth" as the diarist Evelyn called him, more interested in working out and demonstrating problems than in publishing his results. Yet it was his concern with the tangible and visible truths of disciplines such as anatomy, optics and geometry that led him to explore both the theoretical and the practical bases of the early and mid seventeenth-century buildings of Oxford, and ultimately to take up architecture himself. By the autumn of 1661 he was advising the King on the repair of the old St Paul's; two years later he was concerned with the designs of Pembroke College Chapel, Cambridge, for his uncle Matthew, Bishop of Ely, and of the new academic theatre given to Oxford by his friend Archbishop Gilbert Sheldon. The Sheldonian Theatre, built in 1664-9, shows Wren's originality in reconciling the Latinity taken for granted by Renaissance architects with the unprecedented problems raised by a kind of building never imagined by the Ancients.

It must have been in Oxford in the 1650s that Wren acquired a taste for, and a habit of, looking at architecture, and also began to apply Baconian scepticism to the writings of the ancient Vitruvius and the architects and theorists of the Renaissance. His conviction that these, as much as the literature of the sciences, must be tested by a return to first principles, was to be of great significance in the long process between his first proposals for the repair of old St Paul's in the summer of 1666 and the definitive design of nine years later.

It is possible that without the Great Fire Wren would have been no more than the first of a number of Oxford academics who engaged in architectural design as a hobby. Nevertheless by 1665 he was sufficiently concerned with the pursuit to make an extended visit to Paris and the Ile-de-France. His advance contacts were naturally scientific ones, but the two celebrities we know he planned to meet were contemporaries of his father, the French architect François Mansart and the papal architect and sculptor Gian Lorenzo Bernini. Wren certainly met the latter, as well as a number of French and Italian architects and engineers who gave him valuable advice. Paris also introduced him to an entirely novel form, the dome, of which there were several examples although there were as yet none in England.

In the event, by 1670 he found himself, as Surveyor of the King's Works, potentially the most important and influential architect in England — and also surveyor to the new commission set up to rebuild the London City churches destroyed in the Great Fire. He was not officially architect to St Paul's until 1673, but a model had already been made to his first design. Although he would never abandon his scientific interests, architecture would thenceforth occupy most of his attention. Other commissions followed, almost all in public architecture which interested him more than the design of houses. He had overall responsibility for nearly fifty churches. One of his most notable and beautiful buildings, the new library of Trinity College, Cambridge, was begun at the same time as the final design for St Paul's.

In the early 1680s he designed the Royal Hospital at Chelsea and a palace at Winchester (never finished) for Charles II; in these works he met for the first time the problems of scale in large masses of building. For James II he designed a major addition to Whitehall Palace (destroyed in the fire of 1698) and for William and Mary he built, between 1689 and 1701, the great half-palace that gives Hampton Court its present character. From 1694 onwards he was also concerned with another royal hospital, the naval counterpart at Greenwich of the soldiers' home at Chelsea. In 1698 Wren made, and apparently himself drew out, a grandiose scheme for a new Whitehall Palace; nevertheless he was then in his late sixties and although retirement was far from his mind he was beginning to delegate work to younger colleagues, in particular to his pupil and former personal clerk, Nicholas Hawksmoor (1661/2-1736), whose activity in the Cathedral drawing office is both discernible and documented from the early 1690s onwards.

After about 1710, the date of the official completion of St Paul's, Wren became increasingly frail physically, but his mental powers seem to have been unimpaired. Nevertheless there were allegations of incompetence and irregularity which prepared the way for his shabby dismissal in 1718 from the royal surveyorship, to be replaced by the ambitious and quite incompetent amateur William Benson. Accepting his enforced retirement, he removed to a house on the green at Hampton Court from the Surveyor's official residence at Scotland Yard in which he had probably lived for the whole of his term of office. There is no substance for the legends that he ever lived either in Walbrook in the City or on the South Bank opposite St Paul's.

In his last years either Wren or his son leased a house in St James's Street, and it was there that he died on 25 February 1723. Tradition has it that he was making an annual visit to his greatest building and that he died in his sleep after dinner; what is certain is that he was buried on 5 March in the crypt of the Cathedral, near a tablet inscribed *Si monumentum requiris, circumspice* (If you are expecting his monument, look around you).

Wren's library, with that of his son, was auctioned in 1748, followed the next year by over 900 architectural drawings that had remained in his personal possession. About half of these are now in the Library of All Souls, Oxford; those belonging to the Cathedral probably also came from the sale, but Wren and his staff must have made a great number of other drawings that have not survived.

The drawings and their history

The St Paul's collection comprises the greater part of the surviving drawings for the design and construction of Wren's Cathedral. In the past sixty years they have been better known and more often studied through the plates of the *Wren Society* than in the originals; in consequence those drawings never reproduced have been insufficiently studied. The decision of the Dean and Chapter to place them on deposit in the Guildhall Library has meant that for the first time there is adequate space, supervision and security for them to be properly studied during working hours. The present catalogue is thus based on first-hand study of all the originals. It is intended to be as useful to those without access to the originals as to visitors to the Guildhall; it is also an attempt to enhance a physical description by placing the drawings in a more meaningful context and arrangement than has hitherto been possible.

In October 1982 the Cathedral Librarian discovered in a cupboard what is probably the original paper in which the drawings came to St Paul's library: a roll inscribed "A Collection of Drawings great part of which seem to have been made use of at the building St Paul's Cathedral, London". It also gives the information that the drawings were bought in 1767 "for the use of that Fabrick" by the "surveyor, treasurer and paymaster thereof Robert Mylne" from a printer named Strahan who had them from the estate of Mr Grover, a clerk to the House of Commons. Mylne was Surveyor to the Cathedral from 1766 to his death in 1811. At a later date the drawings were pasted into two large volumes and numbered consecutively; this arrangement was retained and recorded in the summary catalogue included in Volume XX of the *Wren Society* (1943). By 1956, when I first saw them, the volumes had been broken up and the drawings mounted on cards. A few had been framed for display, and some had lost their original numbers.[1] More recently, sheets with sketches or inscriptions on the back have been lifted to make these accessible.

This collection ran to 185 numbered items; the fact that they were numbered consecutively meant that after they were re-mounted the volume numbers were superfluous – a fortunate circumstance in view of the arbitrary way the drawings had been arranged. In many cases one number served for a page containing several sheets, some of them unrelated in subject or date. Moreover, the drawings were distributed into two sequences as if there were a division of spoils; each volume contained a similar selection of subjects, so divided up as to separate sheets that obviously belonged together. Both volumes, for instance, ended with decorative details and designs for the organ case.

These irregularities of numbering and classification encouraged the decision to make a new and more significant arrangement, while retaining the original numbers for cross-reference as "inventory numbers". Further impetus was given by the supplementary deposit of the 32 drawings acquired from the sale of the Bute Collection in 1951.[2] These had never been mounted, and when the Whitechapel Art Gallery requested the loan of some of them for the 1982 Wren exhibition there was apparently nobody on the Cathedral staff who could locate them. Their rediscovery in a neat brown paper package received press coverage more appropriate to a scholarly discovery than to a spring cleaning exercise; as a result all 32 were mounted and shown at Whitechapel and then joined the older collection in the Guildhall.

Two other drawings (Nos. 158 and 164) had been presented to St Paul's by the R.I.B.A. in the 1930s, making the total number of items 229. But of the original 185 items 23 were engravings. Only one of these, an annotated proof, is included in this catalogue, and several are still at St Paul's. Most of them are duplicated in the Guildhall's print collection. Subtracting all but one of the prints and adding those drawings originally bracketed under one number, the total of entries in this catalogue comes to 220. Twelve (Nos. 209-220) are later drawings or for other projects, and ten (Nos. 1-10) are connected with Wren's earlier designs for the Cathedral; the remaining 198 relate directly to the Definitive design on which construction began in the summer of 1675. There is a smaller, but extremely important, collection of drawings for St Paul's in the Wren Collection at All Souls, Oxford (mostly in Vol. II). These include the Pre-fire project (1666), the Greek Cross (1672) and the Warrant design (1675) as well as several highly finished drawings for the Definitive design and a few which have the same mixed character as the St Paul's collection.

The history of the design

In essentials the history of the designing and building of St Paul's is well known, and it can be found with varying degrees of accuracy and comprehensiveness in many published ac-counts.[3] Nevertheless presumption should not be made on the catalogue user's familiarity with the subject; moreover, further study of the drawings continues to add to the details of the story.

When work began on the site, Wren had been concerned with designs for St Paul's for nine

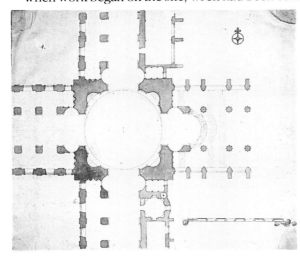

I   Pre-Fire Design (1666): plan
(All Souls II.4)

II Pre-Fire design: elevation with
    cross-section (All Souls II.6)

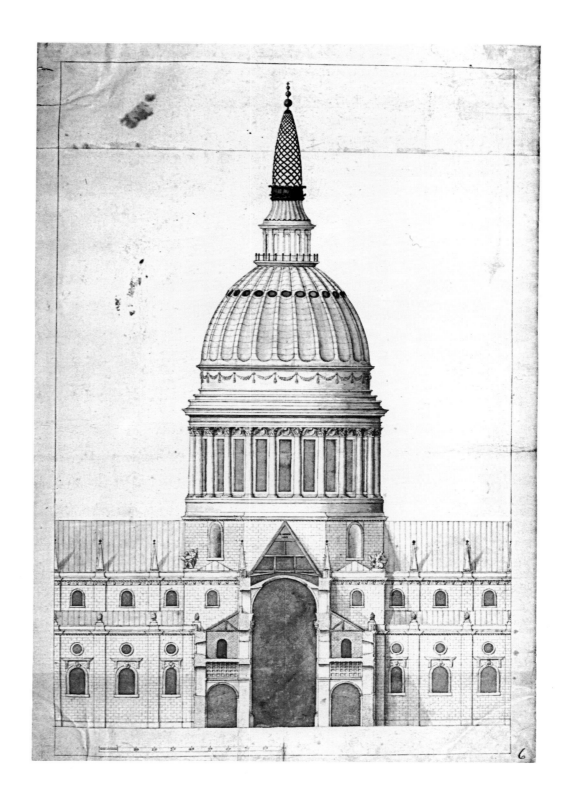

III Pre-Fire design: cross-section,
     west-east (All Souls II.7)

years, that is from the spring of 1666 before the Great Fire of 2-5 September. In May he had
submitted a proposal, and in August drawings, for a new domed crossing to the medieval
building, intended to continue the process of improvement begun in the 1630s by Inigo
Jones, and to give the City of London a new landmark of modern form in place of the decaying
gothic tower which had lost its leaded spire more than a century earlier. This Pre-fire design

14

was made irrelevant by the fire, but it already embodied some of the visual and structural ideas found in the building we see today.

Subsequently Wren worked in detail on no less than five designs in succession. Some of these discarded projects can be seen as experiments that helped him and the Cathedral Chapter to see what they did not want; others may be seen as developments of previous projects. In one way or another each contributed either negatively or positively to the final concept. Probably no English cathedral previously had been designed entirely by one man; certainly none had been completed to one man's design and in his life-time. It is one measure of Wren's stature that, blessed with the life-span and also the tenacity to do so, he carried the whole project through without losing sight of the aims, visual and structural, towards which he was working. Two factors made his achievement even more remarkable. First, the Definitive design was constructed without a wooden model, which was unusual at the time for so complex an undertaking: only a few people besides the architect had any idea of how it was to look or how it was to be built. Secondly it is, as the drawings show, far more complex in design and construction than any of the earlier projects. Its full *understanding* requires a developed capacity for perceiving and remembering three-dimensional structures; its *invention* was only made possible by a truly exceptional capacity.

Wren's first idea for a new cathedral after the fire, blocked in within a few days on a plan for a new city, showed only the basic elements of a large domed space, a square nave or vestibule and a western portico. There followed nearly two years of hardship and pessimism in London, during which the clergy believed that the old ruins could be propped up and re-roofed. Wren's very practical doubts of this were justified by a fall of masonry in April 1668, and he was asked by Dean Sancroft to design a new building. By the autumn of 1669 he had re-worked his little post-fire sketch and rearranged its components into a novel proposal; a wooden model of this was completed in March 1670, and although only a fragment of it survives we know most of its features. It consisted of two disparate parts, a vaulted auditorium, recorded by the roofless model at St Paul's and one drawing[4], and a *western* domed vestibule, which we only know from Sir Roger Pratt's criticisms. The auditorium resembled Wren's own later St James, Piccadilly, but twice as long and with outward-facing loggias in place of aisles under the side galleries. The domed vestibule, which had porticoes facing west, north and south, provided a landmark and a place for ceremonial. This design, consisting of two almost unrelated buildings, was a solution to practical rather than aesthetic problems, and some of the clergy thought it, according to Wren's son, "not stately enough".[5]

He then produced, his son tells us, a number of drawings only "for discourse sake". The carefully finished drawings for the Greek Cross design show a building that would have been a work of art as much as, perhaps more than, a church for use. The First Model would have been the first specifically Protestant cathedral; in the Greek Cross on the other hand Wren aspired for the first time to the scale and the formal qualities of the great Renaissance and seventeenth-century centralised churches of Catholic Europe. The time-lag between his intentions and his patrons' reactions has led to much confusion, and to suggestions that another model was made, now lost.[6] In fact a comparison of the St Paul's records with entries in Robert Hooke's diary shows that the drawings for the Greek Cross must have been paid for in the first quarter of 1672 while the First Model was at Whitehall, where it had been taken for the King's inspection — and forgotten! The Greek Cross drawings in turn received royal approval in November 1672, but the following February Wren told Hooke that a library vestibule and a

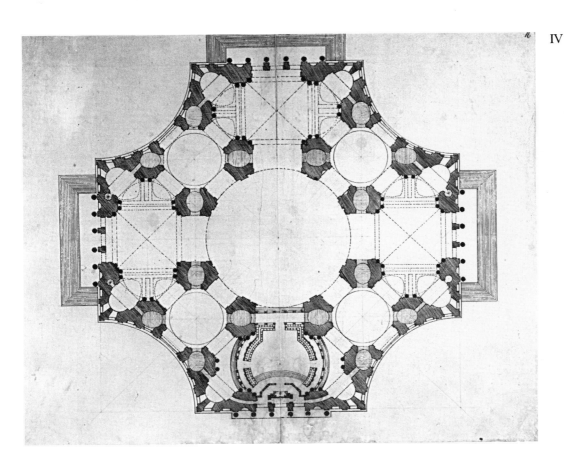

portico had been added to the west end, making in effect, though not without complete re-dimensioning and redrawing, the basis of the Great Model.

On 22 September 1673 Wren and Edward Woodroffe were reported as scaling up drawings for the joiner to build the Great Model, which was finished the following August. Already on 21 February 1674 Hooke examined the interior of it, and on 12 November 1673 a royal warrant had approved the design, set up a Commission for building it, and officially appointed Wren its architect. The reaction of an appreciable number of the Chapter was negative but in the end useful. Evidently they felt it was too unlike the traditional English cathedral of the Middle Ages to suggest continuity with the medieval Church in England as a long nave might do. Moreover, since it was in essence a great ring of eight piers carrying the dome, it would all have to be built at once and no part would be serviceable until the whole was completed, whereas a more traditional cruciform plan could be finished in stages. So far Wren's brief had been expanding; now his patrons were obliged to think and say more precisely what they did and did not want, and thus his brief contracted and crystallised into the set of drawings to which is still attached a short informal warrant dated 14 May 1675, a very different document from the long warrant of 12 November 1673 but nevertheless signed by His Majesty's Secretary of State.

The Warrant design was everything that the Great Model was not. It offered a traditional latin cross plan and basilican silhouette, a dome within and a tall spire outside. Its external

16

V Greek Cross design: west elevation (All Souls II.22)

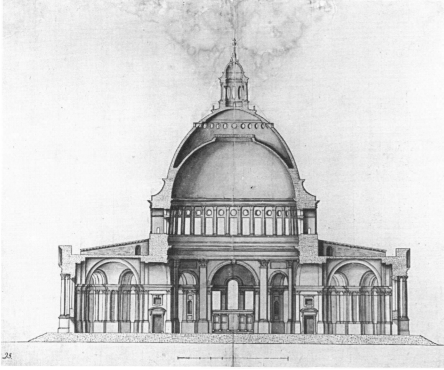

VI Greek Cross design: cross-section (All Souls II.23)

decoration and its western portico recalled Jones's work of forty years earlier and this suggested continuity both with the old building and with the work of England's first Renaissance architect in the previous reign. Moreover, as the warrant says, it could be built in stages. In all these respects it filled Wren's brief, but it would not be a building to lift the soul, and therefore for Wren it could only be a temporary solution. With the private approval of the King he once more set about making revisions: probably nobody else realised how sweeping these would be. In the space of a few months at the most, he re-worked the entire design not once but twice. The first re-working, in which he changed every dimension of the plan, produced the sketches identified by Sir John Summerson as the Penultimate design;[7] the second converted these into the essence of the building as we know it.

VII   Warrant design (1674-5): plan
(All Souls II.10)

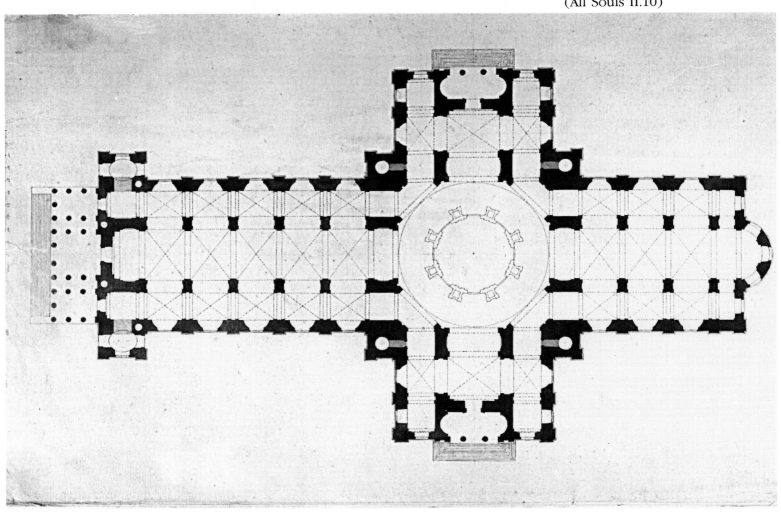

VIII Warrant design: west elevation
      (All Souls II.11)

IX Warrant design: cross-section
(All Souls II.12)

X Warrant design: south elevation
(All Souls II.14)

The final design

How Wren accomplished this process in the time available is still a mystery, which the number of drawings it can now be seen to have involved does little to lessen. However, inventive minds not only react to events that have already arrived but also range into the future in search of possibilities yet to come. Officially the Warrant design was in currency from 14 May 1675 onwards, and officially St Paul's should have been built according to it. In Wren's mind, on the other hand, although he must have considered it seriously when he made the drawings and gave them a title in Latin, the design may already have been obsolete on 14 May or indeed rather earlier. In the light of the time required nowadays for the Secretary of State to announce his decision in a planning enquiry, it is fair to ask for how many months before 14 May Wren's drawings had been on somebody's writing table in Whitehall. Moreover, Wren was not

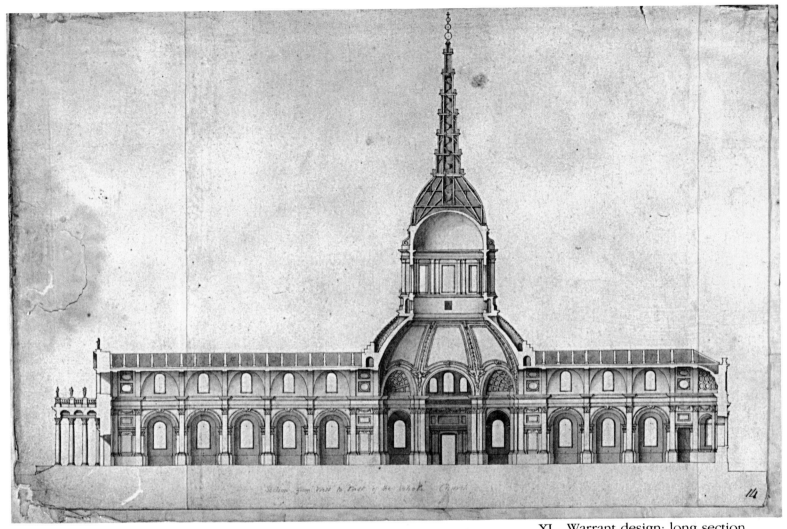

XI Warrant design: long section
(All Souls II.14)

on other occasions averse to the publication of an obsolete design. This would have happened with Greenwich Hospital about 1700 if the proof engraved perspective at All Souls *(Wren Society,* VIII, Pl. XXIV) had been issued, and it did happen with St Paul's in 1702-03 when, to gain publicity and financial support for its completion, engravings *Ex Autographo Architecti* were issued that show a dome and west towers about which he was already doubtful and which he would abandon in a year or so.

When the first building contracts were confirmed on 15 July 1675[8] the design must have been established to the extent of the whole plan, including the transept porticoes and the north-west and south-west chapels, the diameter of the dome and the height and bay design of the screen walls that give the Cathedral its two-storey elevation and provide both buttressing and a visual basis for the huge dome. Wren had in effect re-converted the latin cross of the

XII   Preparation for Penultimate design (1675): cross-section (All Souls II.17)

Warrant to a nave and choir of equal length, with a saucer-domed vestibule in place of the two western chapels. This was well understood in the office, for the accounts refer to the crossing from the start as "the dome" and the vestibule as "the little dome". Only the decorative detail and the dome and towers were subsequently altered from the design most eloquently recorded in a south elevation drawing at All Souls (XIV) which there is a good reason for dating to that year.[9] In 1937 the *Wren Society* editors wrote: "It is increasingly evident that Sir Chr. Wren's design of St Paul's remained fluid until the moment of actual execution".[10] In principle this remains true, but our detailed picture of the building history has changed over the last fifty years, and we perhaps understand better how far the continued growth of the design was conditioned by structural decisions that had to be taken early and which, once taken, were irrevocably embodied in the masonry. The dome and towers in particular represent, in their final form designed about 1704, the line of contact between on the one hand an imagination without limits and, and on the other, a range of statical options that was constantly narrowed by the progress of construction.

Wren's practicality is quite evident in the conduct of the work. The 1675 warrant had specifically commended a design that could be finished in parts, and Wren's constant fear must have been that if some parts were finished others might never be. This is one reason why the choir was not opened until December 1697 when building west of the crossing was far advanced. But it is clear from a reading of the accounts that his concern was not only aesthetic or ambitious but also logistical. Starting masonry work on the western piers of the dome early in 1676 not only made it rather more likely that the dome would eventually be built but also made it a sounder structure: Wren knew enough of statics to appreciate the importance of equal loading and equal settlement time for the whole support. The constant drive westwards and out along the transepts was also good husbandry. Already in his first major building, the Sheldonian Theatre in Oxford, Wren had kept the stonemasons in work all the year round, working stones in the winter and setting them in the frost-free part of the year. In the enormously bigger operation of the Cathedral, he developed a rolling programme, so that, besides the vast and continuous amount of carpentry in scaffolds, bridges, centering for arches and casing for finished carving, such groups as diggers, foundation layers, and builders of walls, vaults and roofs succeeded each other upwards and outwards from the east end. By 1710, when the Cathedral was virtually finished, Wren found himself increasingly in conflict with the commission for building; but in earlier days there were trust, agreement and support. Whatever the implications of the warrant, it was the Commission who in March 1676 gained the King's

XIII Penultimate design (1675): diagonal section of crossing (All Souls II.34)

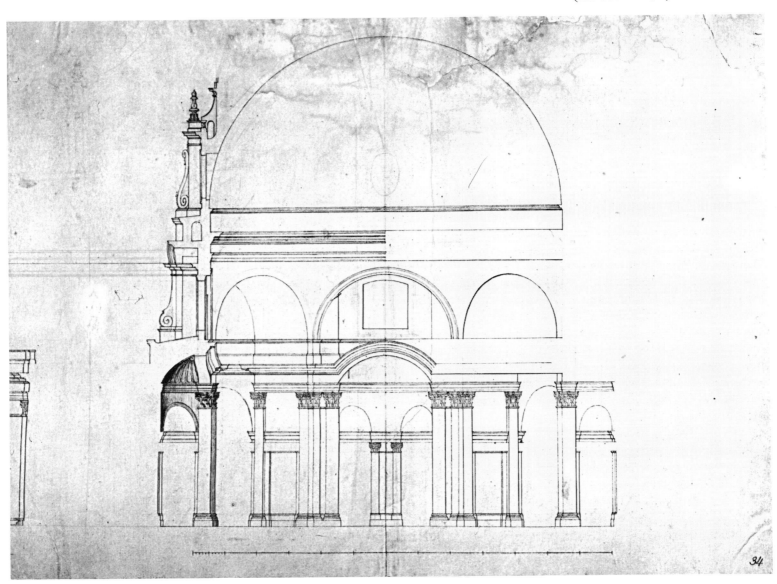

authority to proceed west of the choir and who ordered the extension of foundations to the transepts (9 November 1676) and nave (5 September 1678); in making such decisions it was steered by an executive committee of which Wren was an active and initially no doubt a guiding member.⫽ Much of the Commission's work concerned financial and legal matters, the control of the quarries at Portland, and on occasion problems of broken contracts. But several times Wren was asked to produce his designs: he showed his proposals for fitting up the choir on October 1693 and May 1694, and in February 1700 for the completion of the Cathedral, and the latter exhibition probably led to the engravings of 1702-03. Much earlier, on October 1676 the committee, from which Wren was on that occasion absent, ordered that he should "Bring the Design of ye Church & his Matyes L[ette]r anext to it to this Committee";[12] a week later he did so, and was ordered to "take a copy of the Designs and bring the Originall to be lockt up with the Records in the Office". \

What was "the Design", and why indeed should it be necessary for it to be kept in this way? Wren's son tells us that after the rejection of the Great Model he "resolved to make no more Models, or publicly expose his Drawings, which (as he had found by Experience) did but lose Time, and subjected his Business Many Times, to incompetent Judges". The two minutes of October 1676 might suggest that this secretiveness was unacceptable to the Committee and that he was being brought to order. Surely on the contrary he could only work with them on a basis of mutual confidence. "The Design" was not, after all, to be displayed, or at this date to be engraved and published, but rather locked up in a safe place. In 1681 William Morgan, wishing to embellish his new map of London with a picture of St Paul's, was obliged to state in the legend that "so much as is built was taken from the Work it self" but that "The rest is added according to ye best information we could get hoping it may not be very unlike when finished". It is evident from his picture that very little information was forthcoming.

The rising building itself was wrapped in scaffolding and wattle screens; general ignorance about the design helped Wren to continue or to maintain those changes for which he had at any rate the King's authority. But the safe-keeping of the design was also in part a legal matter. The first contracts, proposed on 18 June and confirmed on 15 July 1675, were for work up to ground level, that is for rubble work in the foundation walls and freestone masonry in the crypt piers. By the confirmation date therefore the plan dimensions and the approximate weight of the walls (and thus the inclusion of the screen walls) were decided, but not necessarily the choice of a Composite for the upper order. The next set of contracts, prepared on 17 August and confirmed on 23 September, were for the rusticated ashlar of the basement walls above ground, and refer to the windows and arches "expressed in the Design".[14] In fact it was quite normal for a builder's contract to specify that he work according to a design, and even for a copy of it to be attached to the contract. In France a special kind of drawing had been developed for this purpose, which showed unequivocally several portions of the whole.[15] Wren had originally proposed the making of a model "for the Incouragement and Satisfaction of Benefactors that comprehend not Designes and Draughts on paper" and for "the inferior Artificers clearer intelligence of their Business".[16] The Great Model would have fulfilled these functions and represented the design clearly for every kind of enquiry; now there was to be nothing more than a folder of papers and, as long as he was there, the architect's word.

"The Design" may have been the set of Definitive presentation drawings which partly survive at All Souls (Fig. 25) and which originally included a plan and a long section as well as

29

external elevations. There are no traces of any similar later set, and it is unlikely that Wren deposited under lock and key the equivalent of the 10ft scale set which followed the Definitive drawings, which comprised only parts of plans, elevations and sections (Nos. 63-72), and which would not be readily intelligible to non-specialists. However, in his own mind and in the drawing office the design was far more complex. It embodied the apparently arbitrary relationship between the interior and the exterior St Paul's and embraced many features that are not shown in the Definitive set, that lie in between two shells and cannot be seen as part of either.

The role of the draughtsman

In fact, while there are some surviving drawings whose purpose or date are impossible to determine, there are many more which can be satisfactorily placed and which tell us a great deal about Wren's practice. Many of the suggestions in the *Wren Society* about the purpose — as well as the authorship — of drawings were wide of the mark, firstly because to its editors the initial value of the drawings was to a considerable extent descriptive: before Poley's magnificent plans, sections and elevations were published the only available sources of such detail were in the early *Wren Society* volumes.[17] Secondly, the editors' mental picture of a seventeenth-century architect's office seems to have been an unhistorical one, and when they did seek out analogies with early twentieth-century practice they drew on romantic notions of the Great Man at Work rather than on practical ideas about organizing people and things. It is also of great and continuing importance to realize that the drawings we know are those that survive, an arbitrary and even haphazard fraction of the total number that were made. If we had, say, 600 drawings rather than 200 our picture would resemble more clearly the complexity of the subject, but also many more questions would be answerable.

Moreover, most if not all of the surviving drawings are ones that were superseded, some were discarded, some never finished. In this lies part of their value, for they tell us more about the process of design than about its final realisation. One reason for this stems from the relative novelty of architectural drawing as a practice in Wren's time. This has implications for the design process itself, which will be explored later, but first of all it is necessary to consider drawings as vehicles for information. The technique of representing a whole building by scaled drawings of plan, elevations and sections was developed in sixteenth-century Italy by architects such as Raphael, Peruzzi and Palladio. It was not only to make architecture reproducible (one of the premisses of Palladianism) but, of more immediate significance, to make it constructible without either the continued presence of the designer on site or the availability of a wooden model.

We are used to dyelines and other photochemical methods of reproducing drawings, but before the advent of photography everything had to be copied by hand. With thin papers some tracing was possible, and the basic points of a drawing — the junctions between lines — could be pricked through two or three sheets at once with a stylus, but everything else had to be done by hand. Late seventeenth-century architects such as Carlo Fontana in Rome and Jules Hardouin Mansart in Paris ran studios on the principle, already familiar among painters, that much of the art could be learned by copying and by drawing; James Gibbs thus learned architecture in Fontana's studio, and incidentally he learned architectural drawing in the Fontana manner. As architecture became more of a profession and less of a craft, and as gradually more aspirants entered studios as pupils rather than as paid trainees, so the presumption of a pool of drawing-office labour became general. For Wren there was no such presumption; assistants who could draw, among other duties and accomplishments, had to be hired or trained, and if there were any final drawings for a building there was only one set. Final drawings do not survive for executed commissions, because they invariably ended up torn, tattered and finally trodden on. At St Paul's, however, the part played by final drawings on the scaffold is in itself doubtful: a typical joiner's payment in the accounts is for "makeing Models & Molds, Templetts &c".[18] Numerous models were also made for parts of the building by the masons;[19] thus while there was no complete model its function as a source of solid informa-

XV   Definitive design: east elevation
(All Souls II.36)

34

tion was diffused into many particular and occasional part models. The place of drawings in the whole process probably came earlier.

Wren indeed had the assistance of draughtsmen, and the question is raised what is meant by "a Wren drawing". Architecture involves delegation, and the concept of a building designed by one mind involves the submission of the minds of assistants to that of the designer. That submission, willingly made, can in itself be exciting and inspiring, as everyone knows who has worked for a great leader or a great teacher. The assistants may wish and even strive to think

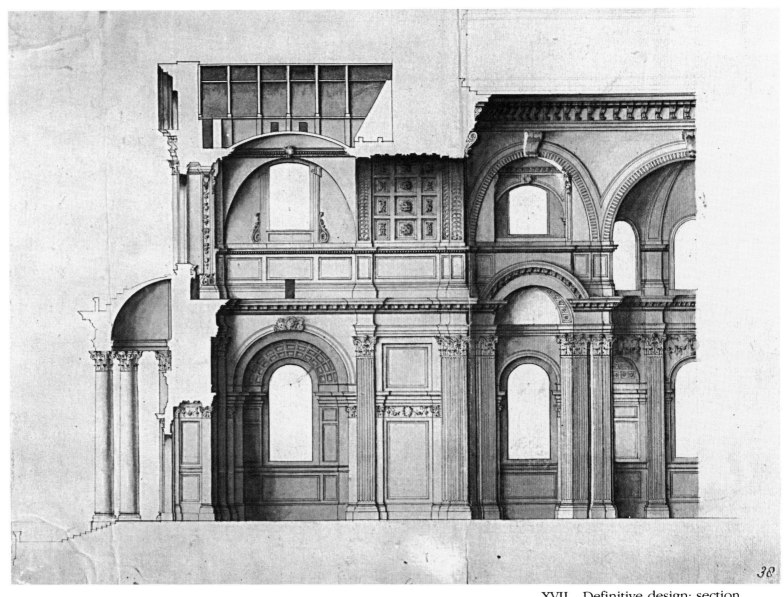

XVII Definitive design: section
through north transept and
apse (All Souls II .38)

and to draw like the master, becoming extensions to his mind and his hand. It is proper to
speak of co-operation or partnership, for it depends on mutual respect: on the master's recognition of the worth of his assistants and of their suggestions, and on their acknowledge-
ment of his individuality and authority. Some assistants never become anything else, either
from circumstances or from temperament; such a person was Edward Woodroffe (1622-1675)
who joined Wren in 1668[20] at the age of 46, worked on St Paul's and specifically on the Greek
Cross and the two model designs, became ill in August 1675 and again in October, dying on

the 18th. His characteristic use of parallel hatching is to be seen in the Greek Cross drawings and in No.95.

Nicholas Hawksmoor, on the other hand, began as Wren's untrained clerk about 1680, remained associated with him until Wren's dismissal as Surveyor of Royal Works in 1718, but also developed his own artistic personality of distinction, not to say genius, responsible for designs and buildings which are patently different from those of his old master. Further, Hawksmoor evolved a unique and recognisable mode of expression in draughtsmanship and handwriting. Yet from 1691 to 1710 he was paid regularly for drawing at St Paul's.[21] While a handful of surviving drawings are without doubt in his hand, another thirty or so may possibly be, but I am as doubtful about them now as I was in the 1950s when I made a catalogue raisonné of all his drawings. We need to remember not only that draughtsmen may cultivate a "house style" but also that drawings are often the work of more than one hand, and that the results may vary with the purpose of the drawing and even with the condition of the instruments used. For these reasons I have been loath to specify hands in the present catalogue. With obvious exceptions such as Hawksmoor's drawings for other projects, Flitcroft's plans and Grinling Gibbons's decoration, they are all "Wren drawings", made under his control and direction. In many instances, not least in the early stages of the Definitive design (Nos.11-42 for example) there are several pairs of similar drawings in which mouldings, capitals, scales and other details are drawn differently, and it may be supposed that Wren and Woodroffe worked together on such pairs.[22] It is a supposition of great value for our understanding of Wren's methods. It gains some support from the phrasing of the report of 22 September 1673 that "Dr Wren and Mr Woodroof has been the week last past in ye Convocation house, drawing the lines of ye Designe of the church upon ye Table there, for ye Joyner's Directions for making ye New Modell".[23] It also helps to explain the existence of a fragment of a south elevation of the Definitive design which seems without doubt to be Wren's autograph — that is until it is juxtaposed with the All Souls elevation (XIX).[24] Neither can be described as a copy, or as better or more characteristic; moreover they differ in many of those details of design (the upper order, the windows at the west end, the ground plinth) which other drawings show to have been undecided in 1675. Similar though less clear-cut discrepancies can be seen in the 1690s for the west portico and choir fittings.

Woodroffe may have come to Wren from the office of John Webb; ten years Wren's senior, he was certainly a man of maturity and experience, and in 1668 he knew more about architecture — perhaps more about design and organisation — than Wren did. During seven years which were crucial both for the Cathedral and for Wren's development their partnership, from very different bases, must have been a remarkable equal one. This seems to be confirmed by Wren's choice, on Woodroffe's death, of another man of years and proven experience: John Oliver (c.1616-1701), a glazier and glasspainter turned surveyor.[26] By the time Hawksmoor was appointed in March 1691 he knew Wren so well that speech can scarcely have been necessary between them, but then Wren was a whole generation older than his assistant and had lived with St Paul's in one form or another for thirty years.[27]

The design process

The paired studies for single bays of elevations, each with small variations, are remarkable enough. More remarkable is a sequence of three drawings (Nos. 43-46; one sheet is divided) for the upper part of the transept end and porch. They are identical in layout and indeed almost identical in content: each shows part plan, elevation and section, and all seem to be in Wren's hand. The layout has the clarity and logic of Wren's diagram of the path of a comet,[28] or indeed of a modern engineering drawing.

Wren's early drawings, for example those for the Pre-fire design, are still as much pictures as diagrams. The change is not necessarily due to the arrival of Woodroffe, but before 1675 it has unquestionably taken place. These drawings of the transept end have the same character as Mansart's contract drawing for the Church of the Visitation,[29] which shows half-elevation, half-section, quarter-plan and quarter internal elevation, juxtaposed on the page as if on graph

XVIII Definitive design: composite
        west elevation 1675-1700 (All
        (All Souls II.39)

XIX   Variant of Definitive design:
        fragment (by courtesy of John
        R. Redmill)

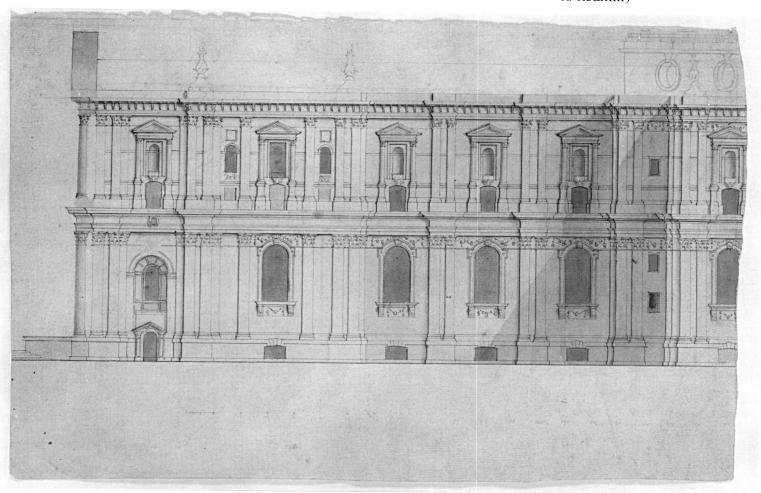

paper. That organisation is one aspect of the transept drawings — and indeed of others for St Paul's — and although Wren cannot be shown to have seen such drawings by Mansart he must have seen a number of architectural drawings in Paris. The other aspect is the very existence of three drawings, all very carefully done, in a sequence of revisions concentrated on the height of a window and the profile of the porch roof. Drawing to such precision, and the expenditure of so much effort on such small revisions, were also new in the seventeenth century. Probably the first architect to work in this way was Francesco Borromini, some of whose plans for San Carlo alle Quattro Fontane have two or three ideas, each carefully drawn out, superimposed one on another. It would be foolish to suggest any direct connection, but a few points can be made. First, there are also drawings by Mansart of this kind, in particular a plan for the Château of Blois, so complex in the overlaying as to be now indecipherable; this brings us back to France. Secondly, Borromini developed the use of the pencil or fine chalk for such exploratory drawings, and Wren and his office on occasion used pencil in this way (Nos. 93, 166). Thirdly, Wren met in Paris not only Mansart and Bernini but, by his own account, other Italians expert in the problems of vaults and domes. With his lifelong interest in drawing and his quick perception, he would have taken note of any drawings and graphic techniques that came his way.

The number and range of drawings for St Paul's that must be placed before the autumn of 1675, or before the commencement of work, shows the importance of the medium as a means of refining his designs. St Paul's may have remained fluid in his mind, but that fluidity involved the use of trial and error on the drawing-board to get the right effect. In his first *Tract* Wren vacillates between the primacy of geometry as the basis of his art and the necessity for architecture to look right — between principle and practice. It may be significant that there are no surviving drawings based on geometrical diagrams, and that although he was prepared to apply such schemes hypothetically to lost monuments of Antiquity, modern attempts to do the same to his buildings always seem to fail against the evidence.[30]

Architecture involves the reconciling of all the conditions of the brief presented; sometimes is is like placing the guests at an embassy dinner party, and the consequences of a false move may be similarly momentous. In the final version of St Paul's dome Wren returned to a 32-bay colonnade which he had already considered in 1675 and rejected; indeed he returned to heights and profiles he had conceived before the Great Fire. There were occasions in the cataloguing of the St Paul's drawings when the story seemed to go backwards. Wren would not be human if he always knew his own mind; what matters is that he knew it at the moment when the builders needed to know it too.

Note: recently three small studies (a half section and two quarter plans) derived from Santa Sophia were discovered in a book once belonging to Robert Mylne, who noted that they were "found among Mr Flitcroft's papers when sold in 1773, and then among some Drawings of Sir Christopher Wren". In style, and in the manner of setting out the structure, the section in particular bears comparison with Cat. 91 (Hugh Pagan Ltd., Richmond, Catalogue 3, June 1988, where the Islamic crescent finial is wrongly identified as a weathercock and attributed to Wren's invention).

NOTES

1 Confusion occurred between Nos. 112 and 172, 121 and 127, and 126 and 169.

2 Sotheby, 23 May 1951, lots 1-3. Catalogued by Sir John Summerson.

3 The most recent account is in K. Downes, *The Architecture of Wren* (London 1982). J. Lang, *Rebuilding St Paul's* (Oxford 1955) tends to omit dates in the interest of a fluent narrative. See also M. Whinney, *Wren* (London 1971). The catalogue of the 1982 Wren exhibition at the Whitechapel Art Gallery contains material not easily found elsewhere.

4 Worsley Collection, Hovingham. Published by N. Lynton, Burlington Magazine, XCVII (1955), pp. 40-44. In a letter (*ibid.* p.120) Summerson suggested that the drawing is an 18th-century copy: Thomas Worsley was Surveyor-General of Works 1760-78. Since examining it in the original at the Whitechapel exhibition I am inclined to agree with this suggestion, which of course scarcely reduces the importance of the drawing.

5 C. Wren, *Parentalia* (London 1750), p.282.

6 This idea was proposed by V. Fuerst in 1956 on the basis of a total misunderstanding of both documents and accounts, and hinges on the number of porters required to carry the First Model from Whitehall back to St Paul's. Trade Union rules of today would fairly certainly demand the four who were provided as a minimum. A recent attempt to revive this canard has produced no new evidence.

7 *Burlington Magazine,* CIII (1961), pp. 83-89.

8 The masons signed them on 18 June but they were not confirmed by the Commission until a month later. There is no record of any foundation stone outside 19th-century legend, and a practical date for the beginning of the work is the payment of 17 July for bringing water from the New River Company's main (WS XIII, p.64).

9 See catalogue introduction to No. 11.

10 WS XIV, p.x.

11 Commission minutes from 1685 on were published in WS XVI; the earlier minute book was rediscovered in 1965 and is now Guildhall MS. 11770.

12 Presumably this letter was the authority obtained in March 1676.

13 *Parentalia,* p.283.

14 WSXVI, p.9 In *The Architecture of Wren,* p.80, I suggested that the rustication was an afterthought though an early one. Since writing this catalogue I have concluded that this is not

so, and that the alternative explanation offered there is the correct one: that on the presentation drawings rustication was omitted as a matter of technical economy. This is confirmed by its absence from the authorised engravings, which were made from Wren's drawings, whereas William Emmett's pirated versions, made from the building up to the parapet, show rustication.

15   The best early example known to me is the contract drawing for François Mansart's Church of the Visitation in Paris, of 1633 (A. Braham and P. Smith, *François Mansart*, London 1973, Pl.111). Ironically, Mansart departed considerably from the drawing in execution.

16   Report to the Dean, May 1666 (WS XIII, p.17).

17   Arthur F.E. Poley, *St Pauls Cathedral*, London 1927.

18   WS XIII, p.124.

19   Two masons took 86 days' work to make a model for one quarter of the dome in January-February 1691 (WS XIV, p.80). It should be noted that the accounts use "the dome" for the whole crossing from the floor upwards.

20   WS XVI, p.190

21   He was paid monthly, as Wren was; both (and others) derived their incomes from a number of sources, the nearest equivalent of which is the concept of the retaining fee, which involves constant responsibility rather than specific working arrangements.

22   Sometimes there seem to be three hands. Cf. *The Waste Land*, lines 359-62.

23   John Tillison to Dean Sancroft (WS XIII, p.51). They all knew each other.

24   Collection of John R. Redmill. Exh. Whitechapel, 1982, No. V.19, repr. p.96.

25   This was suggested to me many years ago by Dr Margaret Whinney, who believed that Woodroffe worked on Webb's projects for Whitehall Palace. "Mr Woodroffe Mason" is named in a draft list of of Works personnel in September 1658 (*History of the Kings Works*, III (1975), p.167).

26   In 1678 Oliver was paid for five years' glazier's work in and around the office (WS XIII, p,114).

27   It was in the autumn of 1661 that Wren was first consulted about the repair of the old building (Downes, *Architecture of Wren*, p.6).

28   WSXII/XLVII.

29   See note 15.

30   One of the superficially most sensible attempts was that of E.F. Sekler (*Wren and his Place in European Architecture*, London 1956, pp.131-7) who sought a grid of squares and triangles as the plan basis of St. Paul's. But when his calculations are checked on a larger plan such as that of Arthur Poley they are full of significant errors.

30. Study for inside transept end. Pen and pencil.

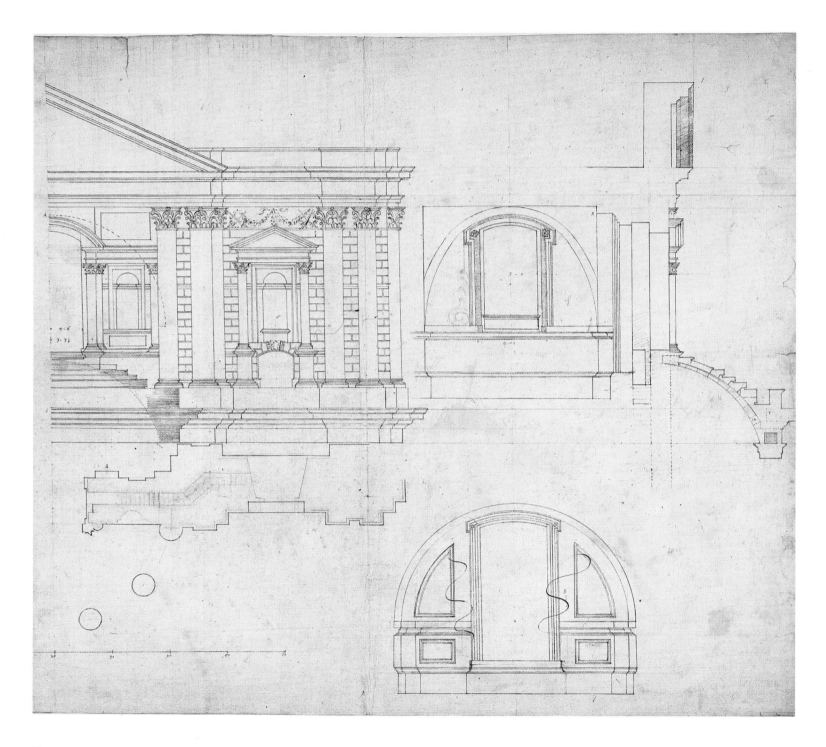

46. Study for upper outside transept end. Pen, pencil
and red chalk.

47. East bay of south elevation, upper storey. Pen,
pencil and red chalk.

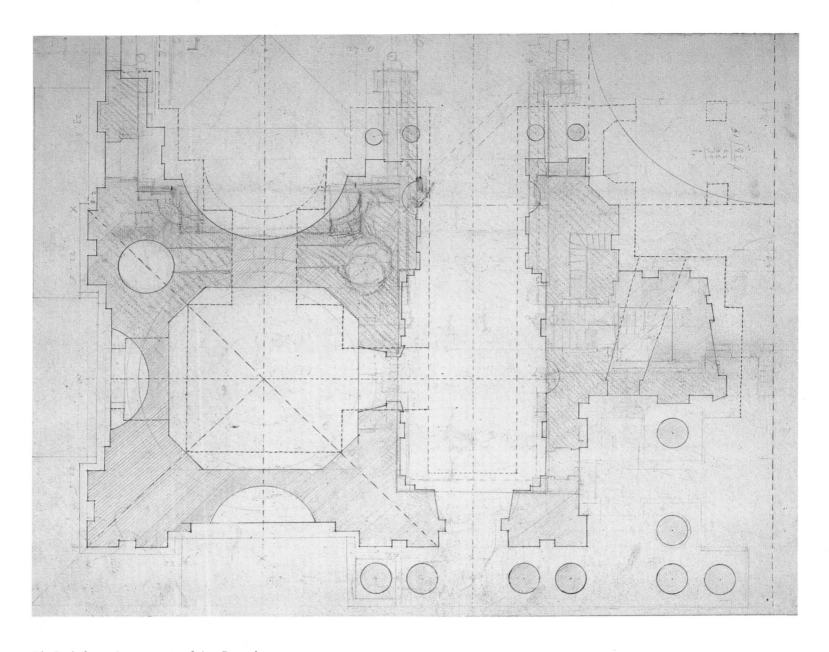

54. Study for north-west quarter of plan. Pen and
pencil, black and red chalk.

66. Section of east end, post-definitive set. Pencil and pen.

41

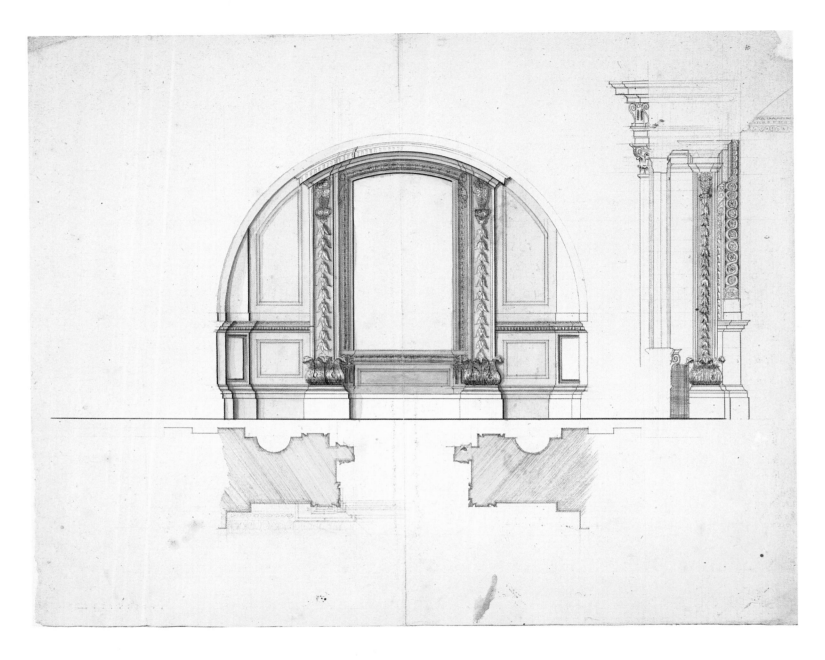

73. Interior study for transept window. Pencil, pen
    and grey wash.

106. Quarter plan of crossing with ideas for peristyle.
     Pencil, black pen, blue, yellow and grey wash and
     black and red chalk.

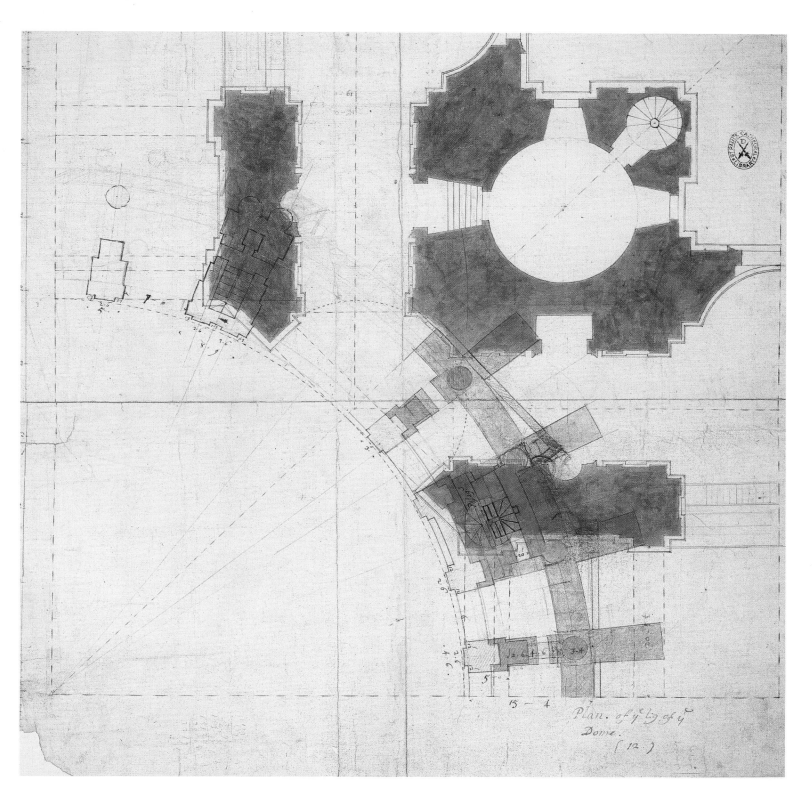

Plan. of y^e by of y^e
Dome.
(12.)

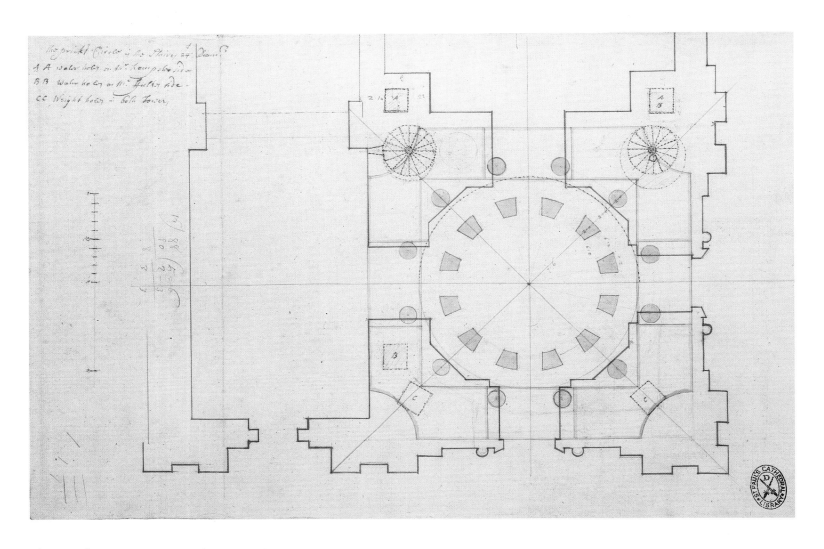

143. Plan of south-west tower, in Hawksmoor's hand.
Pen, pencil and pink wash.

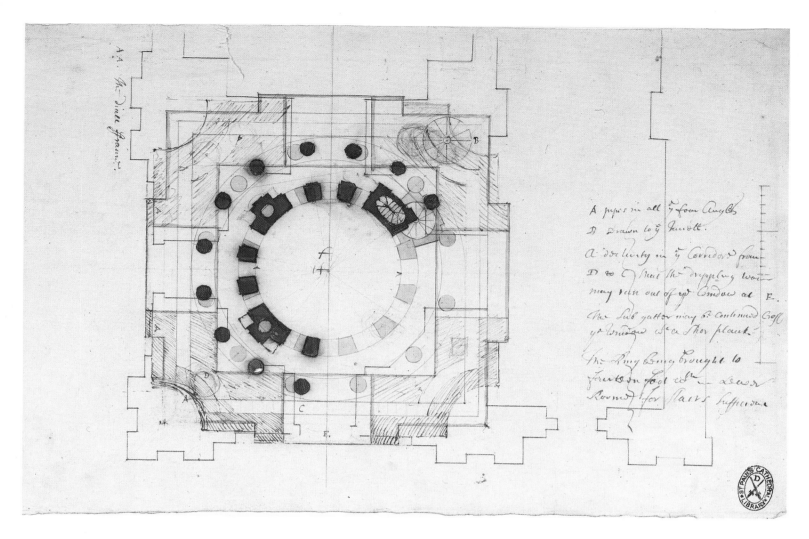

148. Revision of No. 143, in Hawksmoor's hand. Pen,
pencil and brown wash.

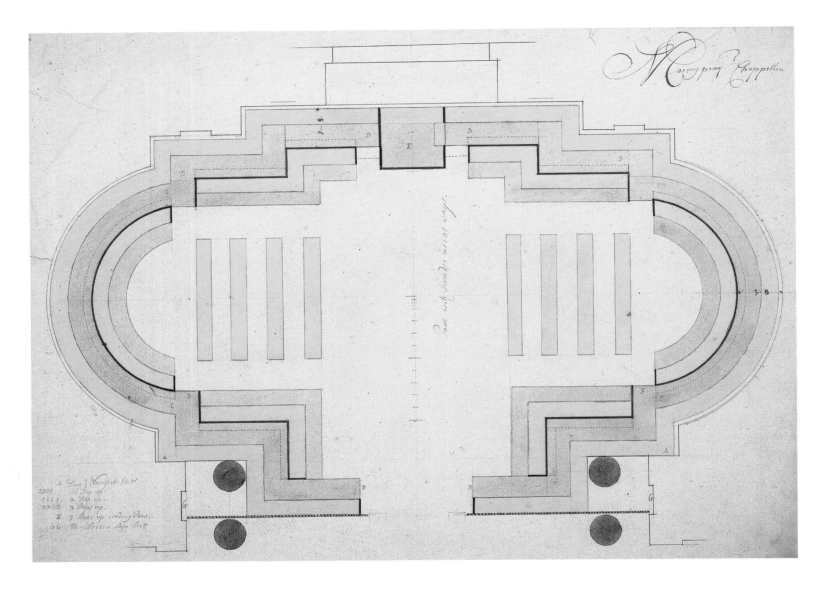

190. Plan for seating, north-west chapel, inscribed by
William Dickinson. Pencil, pen and grey and
yellow wash.

200. Quarter plan of crossing with proposal for paving.
Pen and grey and yellow wash.

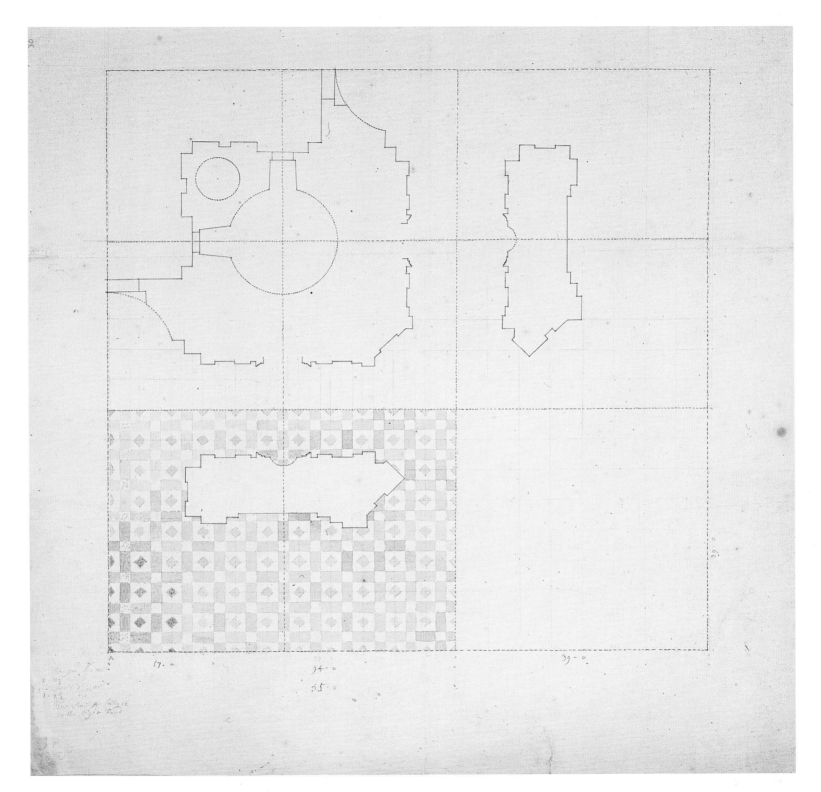

202. Complete paving plan, as executed, probably in Dickinson's hand. Pen and yellow and red wash.

EXPLANATION

Numbering

In each entry the first number is that of this catalogue, to which all cross-references are made. The second (right-hand) number is the inventory number allocated before the St Paul's volumes were dismembered and transferred to the card mounts (SP numbers) or, in the case of drawings from the 1951 Bute sale, the numbers in the sale catalogue which have been retained on the drawings (Bute numbers). In this catalogue one number now represents one sheet unless stated otherwise. At the end of the catalogue is an index from inventory to catalogue numbers.

Dimensions and scales

All dimensions are in millimetres; in unsquare sheets the maximum dimensions are given. Height precedes width. Scales are expressed in feet relative to one inch, or as ratios. Thus "2ft" and "1:24" both mean two feet to one inch. Many scales are approximate, either because paper is dimensionally unstable or because they were set up by arbitrary division rather than from a foot rule. Besides scales of 3ft and 6ft, or 5ft, 10ft and 20ft, others are found such as 7ft and 14ft, as well as 6½ (which may be 6⅔ or one third of 20) and ratios involving the number 11; these include 1:11, 1:22, 1:66 (or 5½ft) and 11ft. A study of the scales of drawings suggested some connections that would not otherwise have been noticed.

Wren Society

Since most writers refer to the *Wren Society* reproductions these are noted and identified by "WS" with volume and plate numbers in Roman numerals. The building accounts were published in Vols. XIII-XV and other documents in Vols. XIII and XVI. Most of the early prints were reproduced in Vol. XIV.

Media

All the drawings are on paper. In general, watermarks have not been noted and no information of value has been derived from this source. "Pen" is used for ordinary pen and brown ink, that is iron-gall writing ink. Other ink colours are noted. "Pencil" may sometimes include fine black chalk, but Cumberland graphite was a standard medium.

Other conventions

Dates are New Style. "Fabric" refers to the completed building. "Endorsed" refers to writing on the back of a sheet. N(orth), S(outh), E(ast) and W(est) are used throughout, as well as L(eft) and R(ight).

CHRONOLOGY

1661   October. Wren absent from Oxford on account of the repair of Old St Paul's.

1663   18 April. Royal Commission for repair. Wren not a member.

1665   Late June. Wren's departure for Paris.

1666   Early March. Wren's return to London.
[7] May. Report to Dean on new crossing.
5 August. Drawings for crossing.
27 August. Site meeting.
2 September. Great Fire breaks out.

1668   25 April. Dean requests re-submission of earlier drawings.
25 July. Order for demolition of old tower and choir.

1670   March. First model completed.

1672   Before 25 March. Wren paid £100 for [Greek Cross] drawings.
June (or earlier). Return of First Model from Whitehall.
2 November. Hooke saw model ". . . approved by the King" (Greek Cross).
9 November. "Curious Model" exceeding old foundations reported (WS XIII, p.xviii).

1673   8 February. Hooke told by Wren of "Addition of Library Body and portico on the west".
Greek Cross becomes Great Model design.
12 July. Sir Roger Pratt's criticism of First Model.
Summer. Scaffolding and standard to set out centre of dome.
22 September. Wren and Woodroffe scaling up Great Model drawings for joiner.
12 November. Warrant for rebuilding commission; approval of Great Model design.

1674   21 February. Hooke walked through Great Model.
8 August. Hooke saw Great Model finished.

1675   14 May. Warrant for Warrant design.
15 July. First foundation contracts confirmed.
17 July. Payment for water supply to site.
17 August. Contract confirmed for above-ground masonry.

1676   November. Transept foundations begun.

1678   September. Nave foundations begun.

1685   Choir and transepts to top of lower order.

1694   May. Commencement of fittings in choir.

1697   9 March. Bill for continuation of coal tax funding passes committee stage in Parliament.
2 December. First service in choir.

1698   Dome reaches Whispering Gallery level.

1699   Cibber's carved phoenix in S transept pediment.

1700   Peristyle floor.

1702/3 Six approved engravings.

1704   February. Final design for towers.

1705   Top of peristyle columns; iron chain; brick inner dome.

1706   W portico completed.

1707   Brick cone above dome.

1708   Outer dome leaded; lantern masonry.

1710   Wren's last official attendances at Commission.

1711   St Paul's declared finished.

1717   Commission decided to build balustrade on church parapet, against Wren's wishes.

CATALOGUE

1. Plan of N half of W portico and vestibule, not as built

BUTE 1

413 x 276   Scale c.12ft

Pen

Limited by the main W-E axis, and cut off on the E where the body of the church begins. Differs in many details from the Great Model; most notably in that the W portico, which in the model is octastyle and projecting, is here recessed behind a screen of six three-quarter columns, flanked by pilastered bays. This would seem to be an intermediate stage between the W front of the Greek Cross drawings and the Great Model.

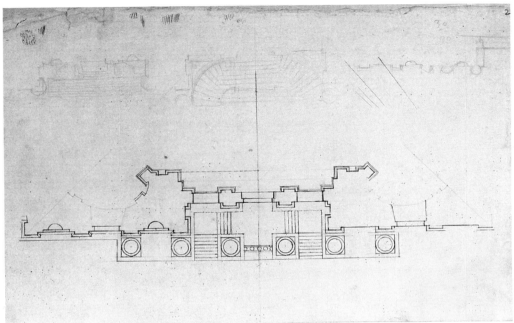

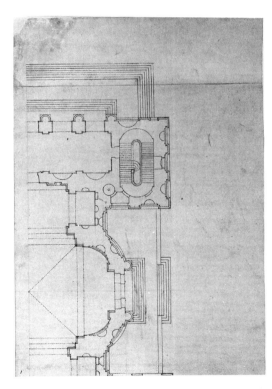

2. Plan study for transept entrance, not as built   BUTE 2

216 x 340   Scale c.12ft

Pen & pencil

Shows L-shaped staircases within a hexastyle portico. The upper part of the sheet has three pencil sketches, two of alternative step forms and one a variant part-plan of the transept end.

Verso: in reverse aspect, a number of pencil sketches: sketch elevation of transept end with segmental pediment, and two detail sketches of the pediment; a square with a smaller one set diagonally within it; part-plan of a newel staircase; elevation and part perspective of a watch-tower with a pyramidal roof.

While in the drawing office the sheet lay under part of a larger-scale plan of the Great Model which was pricked for transfer; most of the prick-marks came through on to this sheet.

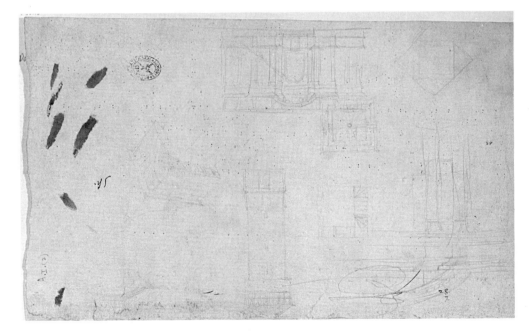

3. Alternative to No. 2, closer to the model
220 x 372   Scale c. 12ft
Pen & pencil
Front with applied half-columns and projecting steps.
A suggestion for a concave central recess is developed
in pencil sketches as well as two small pen sketches
(top R). Turned through 90 degrees, the sheet shows
a fine ruled part street elevation of St Mildred
Poultry, a church begun in 1670 and demolished in
1872.

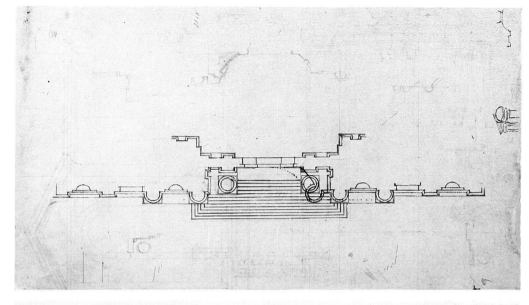

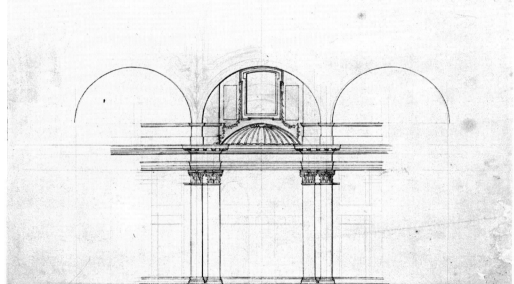

4—10 THE PENULTIMATE DESIGN, 1675

This stage in the evolution of St Paul's, by which the
design recognised by Royal Warrant dated 14 May
1675 was transformed into that on which work began
in July 1675, was identified and named by Sir John
Summerson (*Burlington Magazine*, CIII, 1961, pp.
83–9). As he writes there, a transformation of such
speed "would not be mechanically impossible; but
neither is there any objection to supposing that by the
actual date of signature of the warrant Wren was
already well away with his first revisions". This
hypothesis becomes increasingly attractive as the
amount of work that went into the Definitive design
is appreciated. Wren probably never drew out the
Penultimate design completely, as sketch superseded
sketch. Nevertheless it does represent a particular
stage in his thought, and at least three, probably
five, drawings can be added to those identified by
Summerson.

*4. Developed elevation of a diagonal and two cardinal
arches*   SP 67
235 x 390   Scale c. 11ft
WS II/XXII upper
Pen & pencil
Identified by Summerson in 1961 and described by
him as "preceding the Penultimate". One of its
principal features, before the introduction of screen-
walls, was the large diagonal windows under the
dome, finally to be replaced by the quarter-galleries of
the fabric. The springing of the dome is indicated in
pencil.

5. *Quarter-plan of crossing, dome and transept* S P 14
390 x 257   Scale 11½ft
Pen & pencil
Identified by Summerson in 1961 (repr. as his Fig.
4). The transept only ruled in pencil. The dome has
sixteen sides. Nos. 4 and 5, with All Souls II.34 (WS
I/XXIII upper), formed the basis of the reconstruction
by Leonora Ison reproduced in Summerson's article
and subsequently in the later editions of his *Architecture in Britain 1530–1830*.

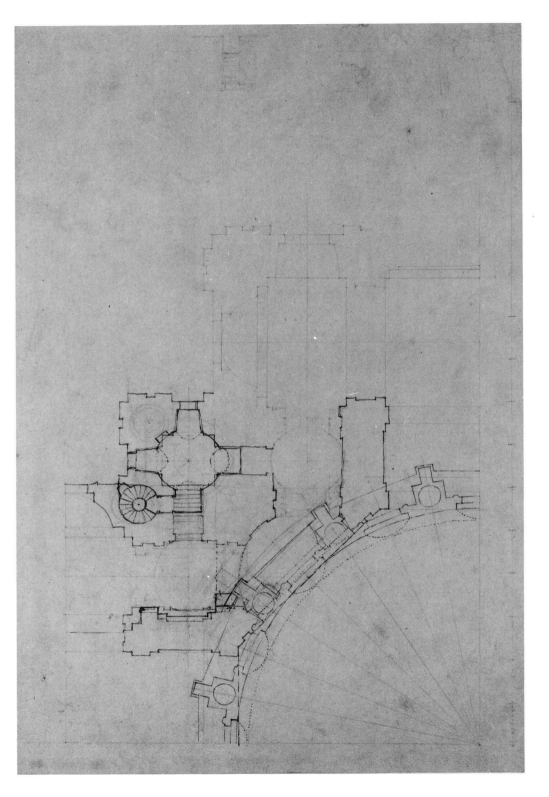

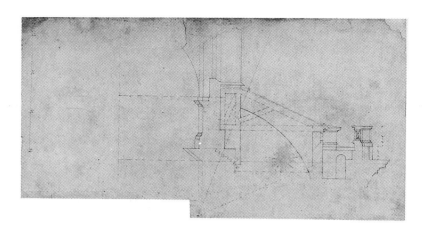

6. Half-section at triforium level SP 133A
222 x 405 Scale 6ft
WS III/XI upper
Pen

As noted by Summerson (1961, p.89 n.19), this drawing is mounted with No. 20 which is to a different scale and not connected in any way. Shows flying buttresses of a lower pitch and triforium roof of a higher pitch than the fabric, and a parapet with balustrade above the first (and here only) order. The only indication of Wren's intentions for the aisles at this stage, but see also No. 30.

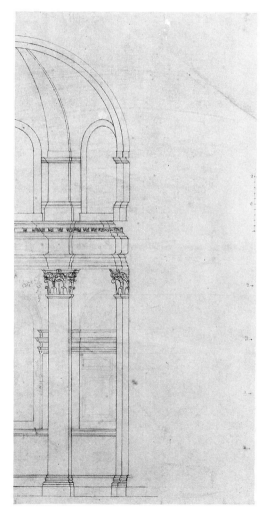

7. Half-section of choir apse SP 121B
460 x 282 Scale c.5ft
WS III/VII R
Pen & pencil

Shows only a single central lower window; other designs from the Warrant to the fabric have three. See also No. 8, to the same scale.

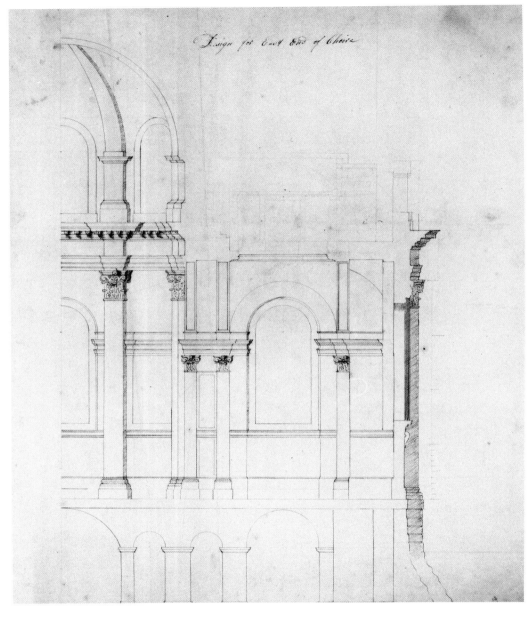

Design for East End of Choir

8. *Half-section of choir*   SP 59

561 x 481   Scale 5ft
WS II/XXI L
Pen & Pencil
Inscribed in a later (18th-century) hand: *Design for East end of Choire.* Repeats the apse conformation of No. 7. The triforium, faintly drawn in pencil, has an almost flat roof and exterior walls which form an attic half-storey. But the triforium seems to have little or no floor: light-lines run from the side attic window through an aperture in the aisle vault or ceiling towards the centre. The full intention is not clear.

9. *Studies for exterior of apse*   SP 48

Two sheets, 146 x 483 and 240 x 481   Scale 5ft
Pencil &, in the lower part, pen
Inscribed in a later hand: *Design for East end outside.* The two sheets, now mounted with a gap, are continuous in design and must have been made to form a single drawing. It is careful but unfinished — appropriate to the Penultimate stage — and certainly early, since even in those details completed it does not correspond to the fabric. Its scale is the same as Nos. 7–8 and its draughtmanship similar. What it does not show cannot be established with certainty, but there is no indication of the screen walls.

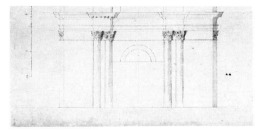

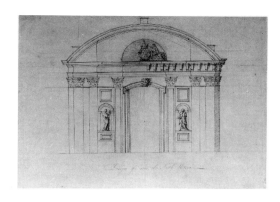

10. Study for upper transept end SP 27
312 x 430 Scale c.6ft
WS II/X lower
Pen & pencil
Inscribed in a later hand: *Design for over the North Portico.* The inscription is comparable to those on Nos. 8–9. Too narrow for a transept end with screen walls (see comment to No. 9). The only suggestion of a segmental pediment in any of the drawings; a triangular one is faintly indicated in pencil. The lunette with the City arms and a R supporter is on a flap, under which are a blank shield and a L supporter. Similar figures were ultimately placed in the N pediment. As in many drawings more closely related to the Definitive design, the upper order is Corinthian instead of Composite.

A finished elevation at All Souls (II.29, Fig. XIV) was dated 1675 by Summerson *en passant* in a *Discourse* on Wren's drawings to the Royal Institution in 1952. In discussions later in the 1950s with Margaret Whinney the original evidence was overlaid by other arguments that were actually less cogent than the original one. Since she remained sceptical (*Wren*, 1971, p.102: "impossible to determine") and it was only during 1978 that the compiler was able to retrieve the original argument, it is worth re-stating. The All Souls drawing is in Wren's hand. It shows a dome of sixteen bays modelled on Michelangelo's St Peter's, but with the peculiarity of piers, not windows, on the cardinal axes. A drawing of an almost identical design with the same feature is in the characteristic penmanship of Edward Woodroffe, who died in October 1675. The terminus thus established for that drawing (No.95) is applicable by association to the All Souls elevation. This belongs to a coherent group that includes east and west fronts (at All Souls) and the lost original of a long section (No.94); they differ from the fabric in many small particulars but only in the upper stages in larger respects. As the only identifiable set of finished drawings they seem to represent the goal towards which Wren worked from the Penultimate design; for this reason the present compiler coined the name of Definitive design.

An early date (not later than July 1675) is suggested by the discrepancies between these drawings and the fabric. The argument that the basement is shown without rustication, for which masons contracted on 17 August 1675, is not in itself conclusive, since even Wren's authorized prints issued in 1702–03 show the walls without rustication. A more serious argument is the statical one: cross-sections of the walls of the fabric show that the foundations must have been designed with the screen walls in mind. Indeed, the whole structure must have been conceived before footings were laid.

Nevertheless the immutability that is practically inevitable in the building once erected, and which is implied in an object such as the Great Model, need not — and surely did not — apply to a design that existed only on paper and in Wren's mind. The process by which St. Paul's was designed is further discussed in the Introduction, but two points should be stressed here. First, that the period leading up to July 1675 saw a great deal of activity by Wren and Woodroffe in the office, which is accidentally represented by the number of extant detail drawings related to this period. Nine of them were not

reproduced by the *Wren Society*.

Second, that at that time Wren was almost literally in two minds about important aspects of the design. For instance, the All Souls elevation shows superimposed Corinthian orders in the two storeys, while the section (No.94) shows a Corinthian small interior order; this and the upper exterior order are both Composite in the fabric. But whereas on the one hand there are several detail studies showing these orders as Corinthian, on the other hand a fragment of an alternative S elevation shows a Composite (see Introduction, n.24) and has various details which imply variously a stage before or after the All Souls drawing. The extant drawings thus represent areas and periods of Wren's thought rather than a simple progression.

11. Half-elevation, exterior of Library SP 31
349 x 467 Scale c.6ft
Pencil & pen
Not as built: Corinthian order; relief panel shapes differ.

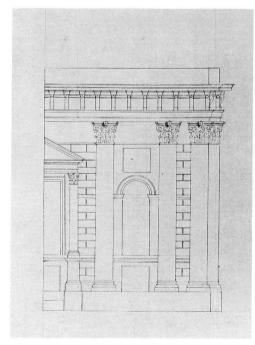

12. Elevation of corner bastion, lower storey   SP 34
294 x 378   Scale c.6ft
Pencil & pen
Unfinished. Inscribed (same hand as No.9): *Break on Left hand side of North Entrance*. Half a choir aisle window is shown in pencil to the L of the order. A gap is left in the rustication for the window lighting the chamber above the vestry, and the shape is not exactly as executed.

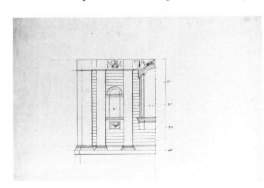

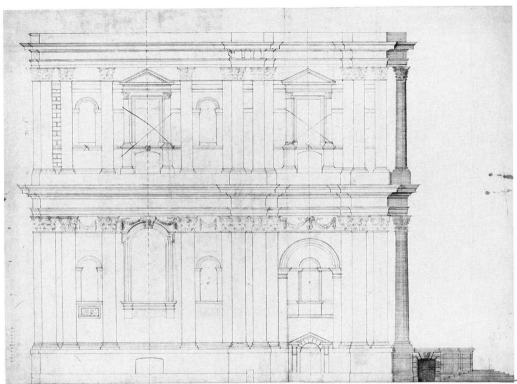

14. N elevation of NW chapel and tower   SP 28
490 x 665   Scale 6ft
WS II/XI upper
Pen & pencil
Double Corinthian order. Triforium-type windows are shown which are not in the fabric or the All Souls elevation, but do occur in the Redmill fragment. However, these features are crossed out. As if in a

revision of No. 13, panels are shown in pencil over the small chapel windows.

15. Study for lower storey, W end of N side   SP 33
346 x 478   Scale 6ft
Pen
Unfinished. Same hand as No. 13 and same stage as No. 14.

13. Half-elevation, exterior of NW chapel   SP 36
320 x 458   Scale 6ft
Pencil & pen
Early: no panel above the small window. No capitals. On the reverse part of the drawing is traced through.

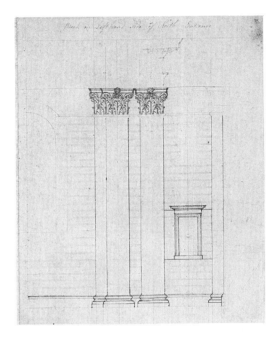

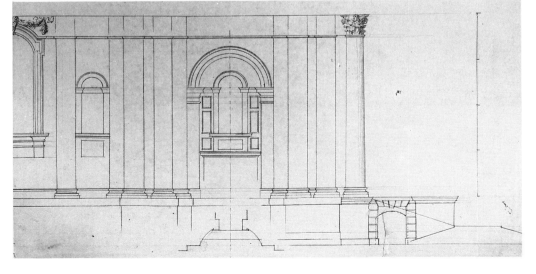

16. W front, S half, upper storey   S P 1 4 4

335 x 418   Scale 6ft

Pen & pencil

Corinthian order. For a similar doorcase to that shown
below the great window, see Nos. 52–53. For a part
N elevation related to this drawing see No. 140.

17. Study of an aisle window BUTE 11
222 x 137 Scale c.4ft
Pen
Cut out of a larger drawing. Probably the earliest drawing of this window form, which Wren seems to have invented. Here the lugs at the top of the architrave have not reached their final form, and the keystone has no cherub-head. The L and R halves show alternative corbels; the lion's head and fluting on the R are possibly a reminiscence of the frieze added by Inigo Jones to the clerestory of Old St Paul's.

18. S choir aisle, E bay of elevation ▶ SP 30
279 x 432 Scale 4ft
WS II/XII
Pencil & pen
Cut L, top and bottom. In the same hand as No. 17 and very probably Wren's. These drawings and those that follow are to uniform scale and in at least two hands, one of which is very probably Woodroffe's. The corbels are again alternatives, and the ornament again probably relates to the drops in Jones's frieze. The half bay on the R is not as in the fabric.

◄ 19. *Study for one bay of aisle wall*   SP 134A
413 x 263   Scale c.4ft
WS XIII/X R
Pen
Variant with a large block projecting from the entablature over the keystone.

20. *Study for S transept wall and portico*   SP 133B
426 x 390   Scale 4ft
WS III/XI lower
Pen
Differs from fabric in details, and no crypt window is shown.

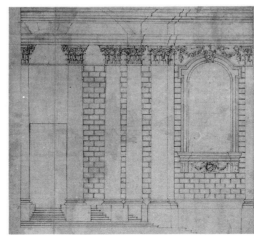

21. *Study for one bay of aisle wall*   SP 134B
417 x 320   Scale 4ft
WS XIII/X L
Pen
Same hand as No. 20.

63

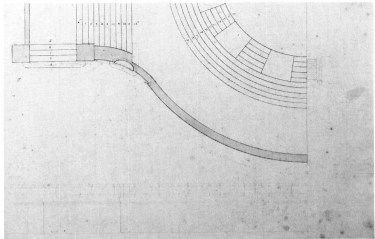

22. Revision of No. 20　　　　　　　　SP 29
458 x 361　Scale 4ft
WS XIII/VI
Pen
Higher off the ground than No. 20 by the equivalent of one course of rustication; this corresponds to fabric. This difference is not maintained consistently in drawings before the sets Nos. 63–73; the All Souls elevation has the extra course but the alternative fragment does not.

23. Half-plan of S portico　　　　　　　SP 9
516 x 362　Scale 4ft
WS XIII/V lower
Pencil, pen & grey wash
The number of steps not as executed. In pencil, perpendicular to the plan, are drawn a section through the circular steps, with the base of a column, and an elevation of the parapet to the podium.

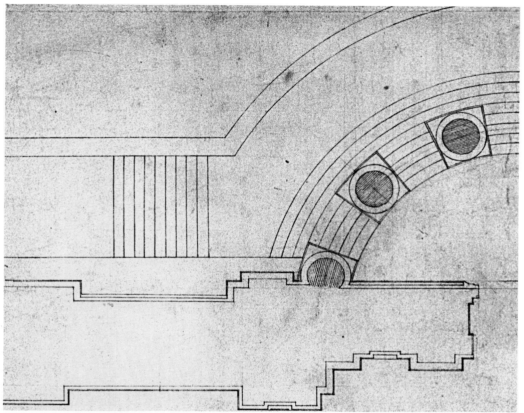

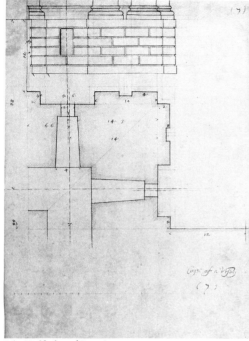

24. Half-plan of S portico   SP 96
355 x 411   Scale 4ft
WS XIII/V upper
Pen
Close to No. 22.

25. Plan and basement front of a bastion corner   S P 38
394 x 258   Scale 4ft
Pen & pencil
Inscribed: *Coyne of a Vestry*. Cut at top but perhaps not
significantly. Close to fabric but lacking the double-
course plinth at the bottom.

26. Duplicate of No. 25   S P 39
362 x 257   Scale 4ft
WS XIII/XVI top R
Pen & pencil
Wrongly described in WS XX, p.37.

27. One bay of basement: elevation, section and plan S P 40
241 x 388   Scale 4ft
WS XIII/XVI lower L
Pen & pencil
As the fabric except for the omission of the double
bottom plinth.

65

28. *Study for attic of apse*   S P 47
344 x 487   Scale 4ft
WS II/XVI upper
Pen & pencil
Inscribed in a later hand (same as No. 10?): *Designe for East End outside*. On the parapet, in pencil, a book surrounded by flames. On the R, a large-scale (1:4) profile of the square die and roundel in the attic centre. Not identical with the fabric; the location at this point in the catalogue is suggested by the scale.

29. *Study for upper storey of apse*   S P 37
431 x 290   Scale c.4ft
Pencil & black pen
Elevation and cross-section of wall bay, not as executed but precisely dimensioned. Trimmed R.

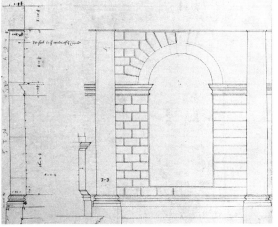

66

30. Study for inside transept end   S P 6 4
Two sheets, 383 x 259 and 379 x 261   Scale 4ft
WS XIII/IX
Pen & pencil
Originally one drawing made of two pieces joined, now separated. Cut except at bottom. This fine drawing and the two following ones are the earliest of this group of studies, for they bear traces of the Penultimate stage (Cf. Summerson, 1961, p.89 n.19). In the section of the outer wall in No. 30 a small vaulted passage above the "spherical arches" of the aisle windows (as the building accounts call them) is shown; this, and the wall above the outside entablature, which looks like a parapet, correspond to

the detail section study of this area (No. 6) which has been identified with the Penultimate stage. However, in No. 30 the outline of the flying buttress corresponds to the fabric rather than the low pitch of No. 6. Confirmation of this relationship appears in the height of the main internal pilaster order, in which the top of the capitals is 43ft from floor level: this is 18ins higher than in the fabric, and corresponds to the Penultimate design. It may be noted that the extra height survives in a later cross-section (No. 51) whose drawn dimensions match the fabric but whose written ones do not. Such inconsistencies are not uncommon in preparatory drawings.

31. Study for inside transept end   SP 129A
410 x 283   Scale 4ft
WS XIII/VII L
Pen & pencil
Unfinished. Trimmed L and R. The order is a few inches shorter than in No. 30.

32. Variant of No. 31   SP 129B
407 x 270   Scale 4ft
WS XIII/VII R
Pen & pencil
Trimmed L and R. The order reduced to 42ft, the details somewhat closer to the fabric. Not the same hand as No. 31.

33. Cross-section through transept doorway   SP 126D
332 x 142   Scale 4ft
WS XIII/XVIII bottom L
Pen
Close to No. 32.

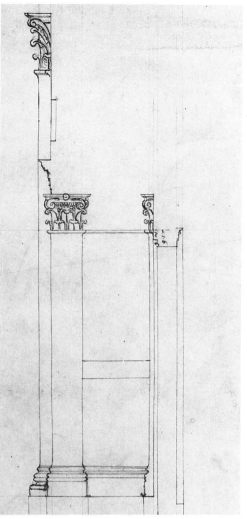

69

34. Internal elevation of a choir aisle window SP 122A
430 x 273   Scale 4ft
WS XIII/XI lower
Pen & pencil
Trimmed R. This and Nos. 30–31 are in the same hand. Close to the fabric; the choir rather than transepts or nave is indicated by the coffering pattern of the spherical arch.

35. Unfinished copy of No. 34 SP 122B
389 x 249   Scale 4ft
Pen & pencil
Trimmed R. In a different hand.

36. Internal elevation, W aisle of S transept   BUTE 13
438 x 379   Scale 4ft
Pen & pencil
Originally identified as the aisle side of one of the
primary crossing piers, but on the L is part of an aisle
window. Of the eight internal faces offered by the
corner bastions only two, on the W side of the
transepts, have niches rather than doorcases.

The niche is shown also in plan. At bottom R is a
faint pencil sketch of a relief with crossed swords.

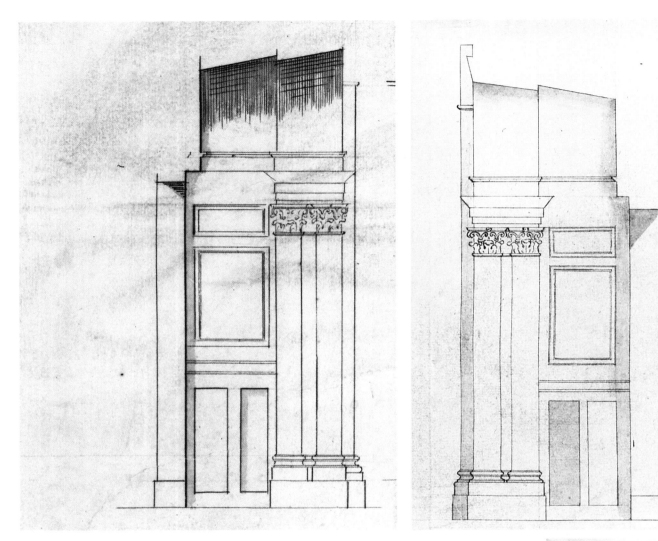

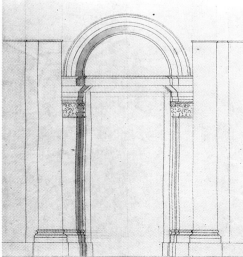

37. Cross-section of W doorway   S P 1 2 7 B
336 x 148   Scale c.6ft
WS III/IX L
Pen
This and following drawings confirm that detailed
thought was given to the W end before the establish-
ment of the Definitive design. The Corinthian small
order corresponds to that stage (Cf. No. 94); this is an
excursion from the Composite of the Penultimate
(seen in All Souls II.34) and Nos. 30–35, to which
Wren returned in the final execution.

38. Cross-section of W doorway   S P 1 2 6 A
240 x 126   Scale 6ft
WS XIII/XVIII top centre
Pen & grey wash
Similar to No. 37 but in another hand.

39. Internal elevation of W doorway   S P 1 2 6 C
237 x 186   Scale 6ft
WS XIII/XVIII top R
Pen & grey wash
Corresponds to No. 38

40. *Internal elevation of aisle W doorway*   SP 125B
239 x 103   Scale 6ft
WS XIII/XVIII top L
Pen & grey wash
Corresponds to No. 39, again Corinthian.

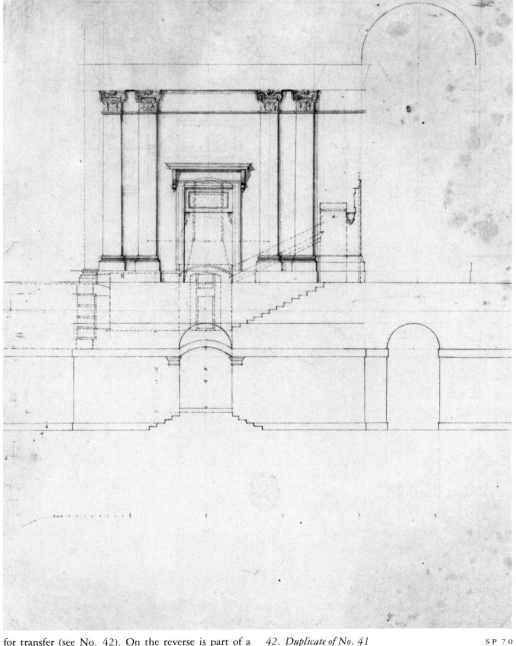

41. *Study of pier, W end of S choir aisle*   BUTE 12
389 x 298   Scale 6ft
Pen
Elevation and section of pier, showing interior order, steps up to Dean's Vestry, and upper flight and bottom steps of stair down to crypt. Roughly as executed, but with Corinthian small order. Pricked for transfer (see No. 42). On the reverse is part of a plan of one principal crossing pier.

42. *Duplicate of No. 41*   SP 70
360 x 269   Scale 6ft
WS II/XIII lower

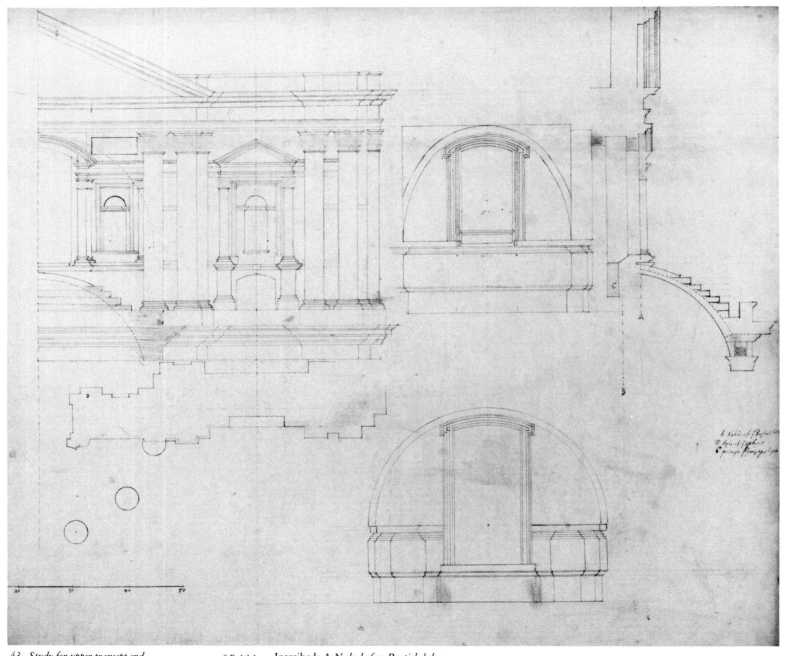

43. *Study for upper transept end*
517 x 611   Scale 6ft
WS XIII/VII upper
Pen

SP 131

Inscribed: *A Naked of ye Rustick below*
B Axis of ye sphere
C passage flying up steps.
Naked can be used as the surface of a wall.

Nos. 44–5 match exactly and formed the halves of a single sheet which was folded and eventually torn along the fold; the two halves were allotted to different volumes. We thus have a sequence of three careful detailed studies, each comprising (a) half external elevation of upper transept end; (b) internal elevation of clerestory window and section of upper end wall and semi-dome of portico; (c) half-plan of transept end wall and portico; (d) internal elevation of upper transept end. We may imagine that similar effort went into the drawing out of other portions of the design, but among surviving sheets these are unique. Some changes were made to (d); even in the last drawing this detail does not conform with the fabric, which may account for its being crossed out in No. 46. Most of the revision, however, concerns the areas covered by the flaps: the aedicule and triforium window which are common to all the screen walls, and the semi-dome of the transept portico and the window above it.

Nos. 44–45 were first drawn as a virtual copy of No. 43, except for the revision of (d). Revisions were then made on three flaps, and these were incorporated into No. 46. In this process the detailing of the aedicule was adjusted and refined; rustication was also added, although its previous omission was probably a matter of convenience rather than of design. The transept window was lowered about 18ins, and the number of steps of the semi-dome visible above the parapet, seen most clearly in the section (b), was reduced from four to three. The upper order in all these drawings is Corinthian. The results of the revision can be seen in the Definitive S elevation (Fig. XIV).

A related unfinished drawing is on the reverse of No. 50. It shows the window still raised but the semi-dome reduced to three steps. It also shows relief carving and parapet statues similar to the Definitive S elevation.

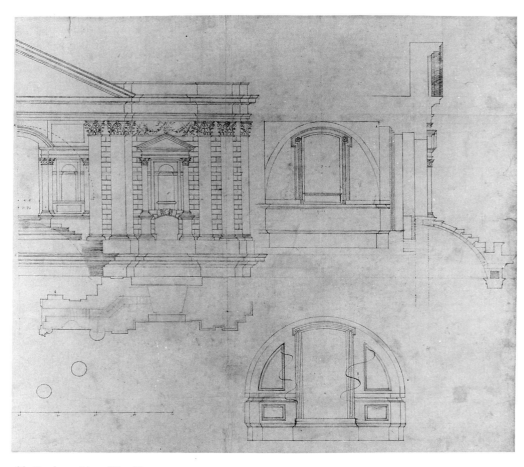

46. Further revision of No. 43
526 x 590   Scale 6ft
WS XIII/VII lower
Pen, pencil & red chalk

SP 132

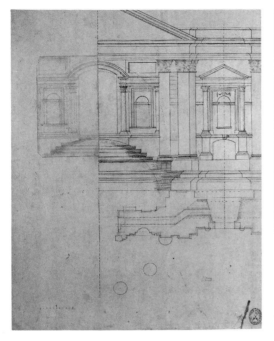

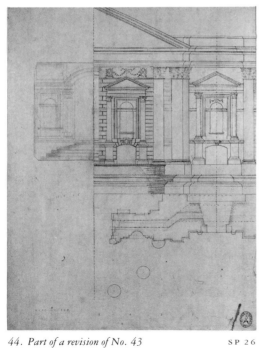

44. Part of a revision of No. 43
482 x 346   Scale 6ft
WS II/X upper
Pen & red chalk

S P 2 6

Flaps with alternatives cover the elevation between
the pilasters.

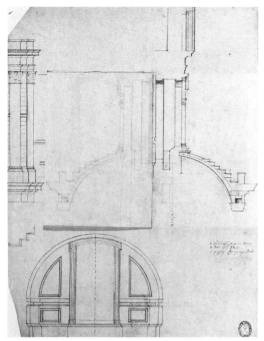

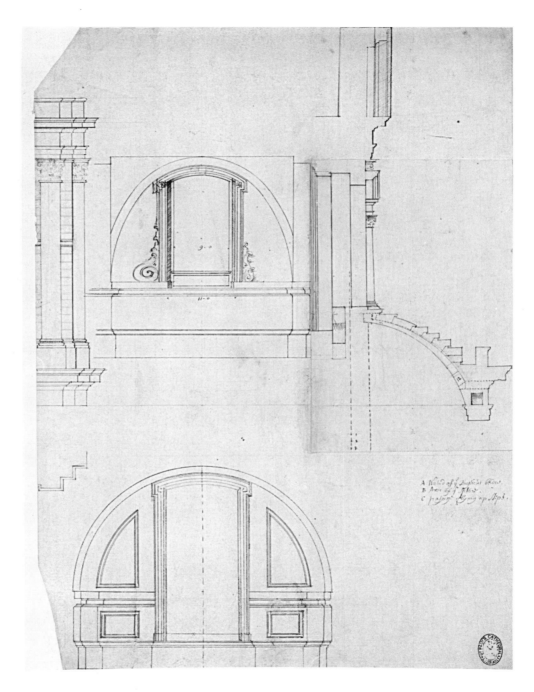

45. The other half of No. 44   S P 6 8

476 x 341   Scale 6ft

WS II/XXI R

Pen & pencil

Cut all round. A flap with an alternative covers the
section of the end wall. The inscription is identical
with No. 43 but a fourth line marked D in pencil is
too faint to read.

47. E bay of S elevation, upper storey   SP 130

496 x 603   Scale 3ft

WS III/X

Pen, pencil & red chalk

Pencilled relief work in the band at capital level has been erased. Corinthian order. A plan of one pier shows the posts that carry the triforium roof (see No. 49).

48. Half-section through main vault and screen wall

SP 114

503 x 681   Scale 3ft

WS III/II lower

Pen

Showing the geometry of the flying buttress and the form of the triforium roof. In the section through the screen wall it can be seen that the triforium window extends down to floor level (the top of the lower cornice); this variation also occurs in the Redmill fragment. Corinthian order.

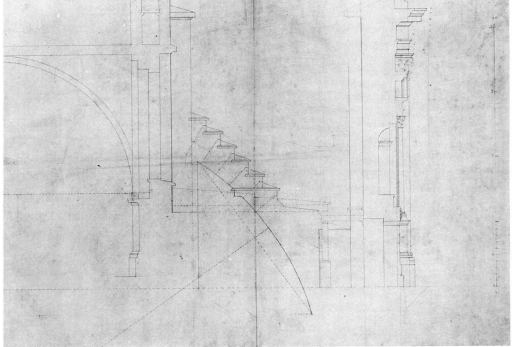

49. Plan of two bays of aisle and triforium SP 98
521 x 285 Scale 6ft
WS III/IV upper
Pen & red chalk
Chalk is used for the upper level wall plan. Probably
related to Nos. 47–48 but at half the scale.

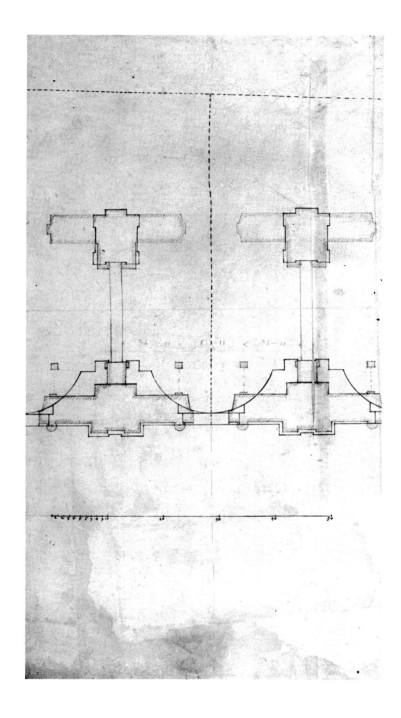

50. *Study section of vault and front of bastion*   SP 35
352 x 454   Scale c.6ft
Pen
A flap shows the window in the bastion closer to the
fabric than to the Definitive S elevation. The order is
still Corinthian.
Verso: in reverse aspect, half-elevation of upper transept end and portico, with section through the same.
Scale 6ft; pen and pencil. Unfinished and partly
deleted, but confirming an intimate connection between the *recto* and studies for the Definitive elevation; see discussion after No. 46.

51. *Half-section of choir showing construction*   SP 115
620 x 446   Scale c.5ft
WS III/VI
Pen & pencil
Presumably for the choir rather than the nave since (1)
such a drawing would be required at an early stage;
(2) there is a suggestion of the lozenge coffering in the
spherical arch, as in the choir; (3) the formal swag on
the impost frieze corresponds to those in the choir
rather than the freer and later forms of the nave.

The upper outside order and the small inside order
are both Composite, and drawn dimensions agree
with the fabric. A series of written and figured
dimensions, however, appear to relate back to an
earlier stage (see No. 30). What appears to be a light-
line pencilled from the top back of the screen wall
through the inside sill of the clerestory window is
marked *att 5 foot high in ye middle of* [   ].

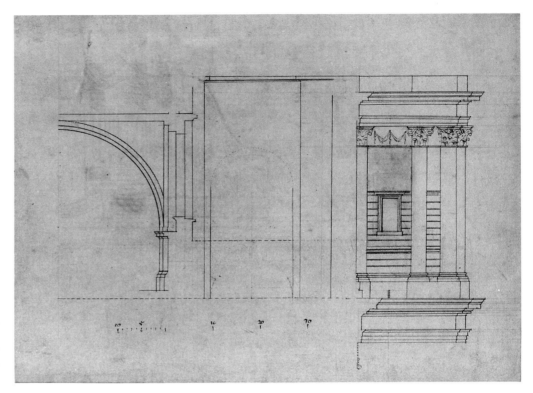

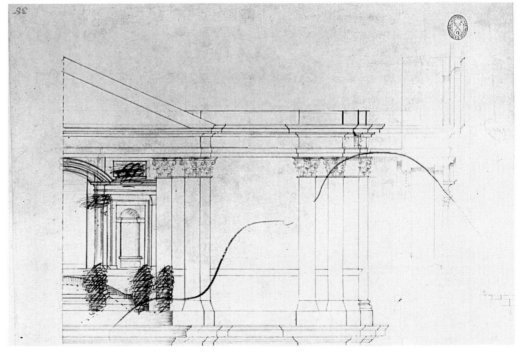

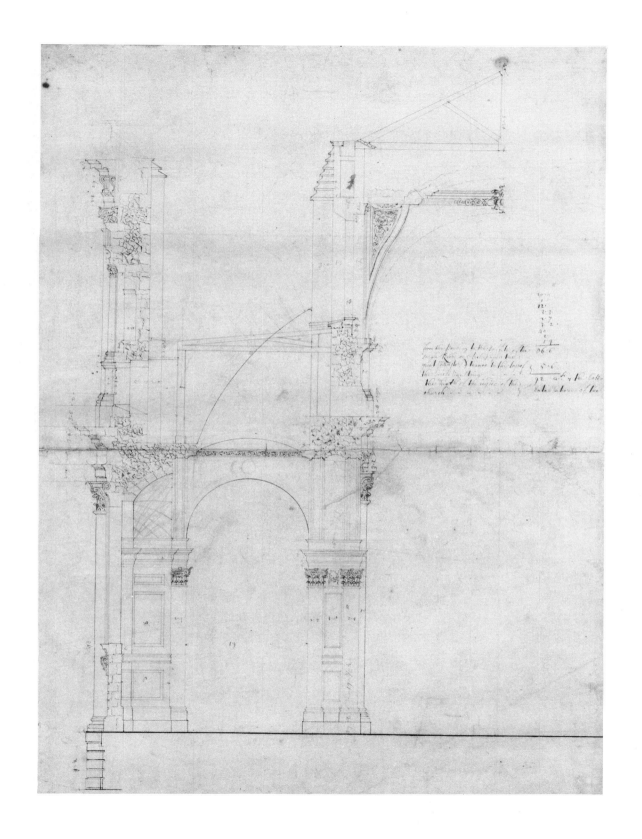

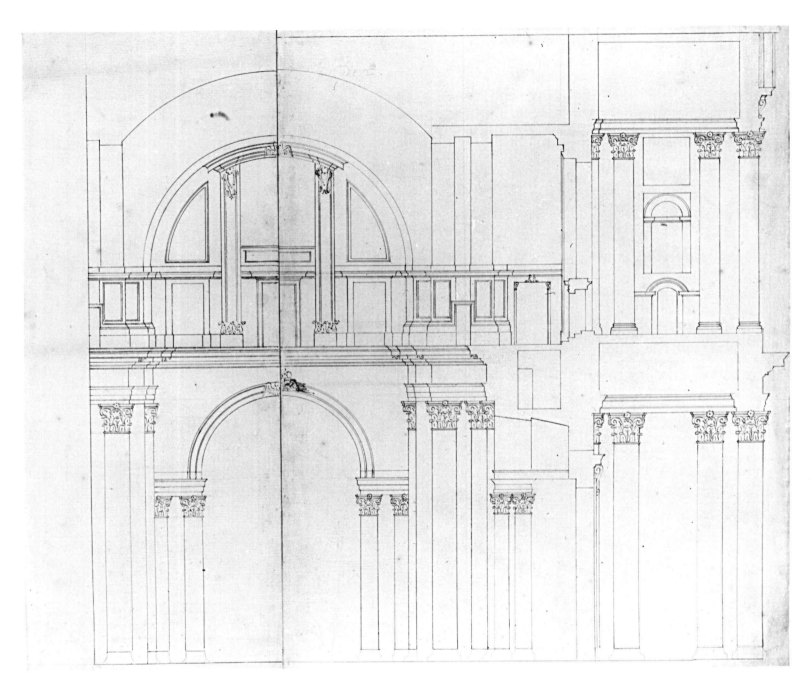

52. Section E–W through W bay and portico SP 63
456 x 520   Scale c.6ft
WS XIII/XXI
Pen
Unfinished: the bases of the order are omitted. The upper outside order is Composite but the small inside is still Corinthian. Two slightly different half alternatives are shown for the domed W bay; the two parts are actually on separate pieces of paper butt-jointed on the vertical axis of the bay. The small door in the upper portico with a segmental head was not executed. See also Nos. 16 and 53.

53. Section W–E through portico and half W bay

SP 127A

460 x 362   Scale c.6ft
WS III/IX R
Pen with some pencil shading
Inscribed under the arch: *A shall project if B and ye other Pannells should not answer those below. A* is the lunette in the portico above the main door. The pencil inscription looks like Hawksmoor's writing and may have been added with the shading in the 1690s to an older drawing which is in most respects a reverse copy of No. 52.

Among unpublished drawings at All Souls (IV.116) is a half-elevation of the upper portico wall with part of the lower wall (below). It shows the same segmental-headed doorcase and must be of early date since the order is Corinthian.

54. Plan study for NW quarter SP 4

437 x 339 Scale 6ft

WS II/II

Pen & pencil, overdrawn in black and red chalk

Plan N of centre axis and W of centre of NW chapel, at crypt and floor levels, not as built. Among other differences, extra columns are shown dividing the porch into three bays, and the centre intercolumniation of the portico is no wider than the others.

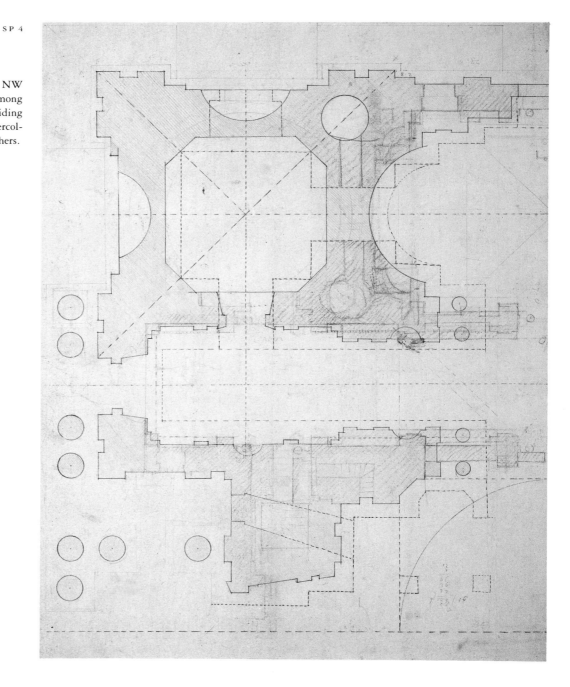

55. Plan study for SW quarter   S P 9 7

542 x 405   Scale c.6ft

WS III/III

Grey pen & wash

Church floor and clerestory levels, the latter shaded.
Two extra columns are pencilled roughly behind the
middle pair. Centre intercolumniation still no wider
than the others; in other respects this plan is quite
close to the fabric and an early date cannot be proved.

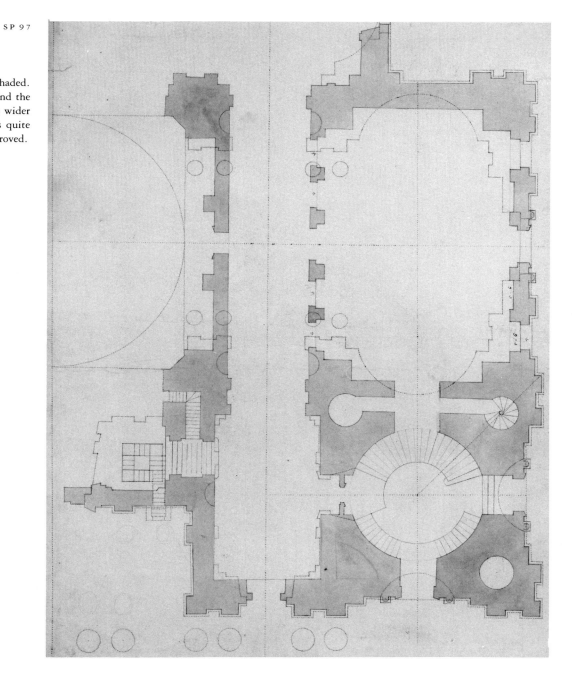

56. Part-section of W bay of nave   S P 1 2 1 A
363 x 230   Scale c.6ft
WS III/VII L
Pen & pencil
A rather free drawing with suggestions for decoration, including a continuous shell dome instead of a saucer-dome with pendentives. An early date cannot be proved.

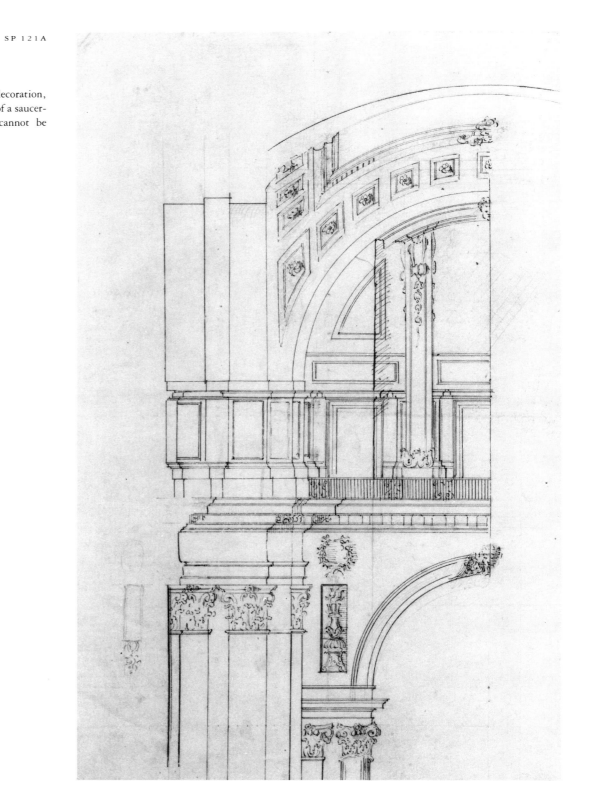

57. *Revision of No. 48*   SP 116
516 x 604   Scale 3ft
Pen, the lower radius line in red chalk
The Corinthian order has been replaced by Composite, but whether by oversight or not the triforium window still extends down to floor level.

58. *Revision of No. 50*   SP 66
310 x 462   Scale 6ft
WS XIII/XV
Pen & pencil
Composite order. The positions of two iron chains are shown.

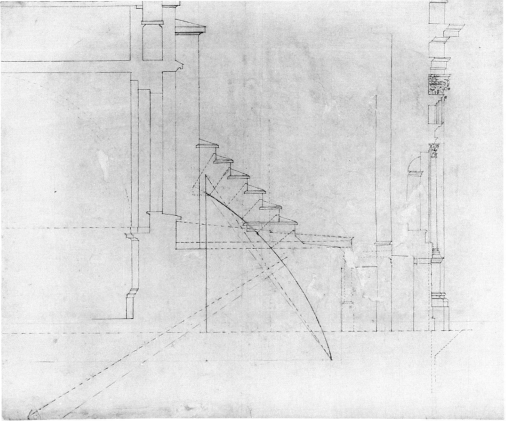

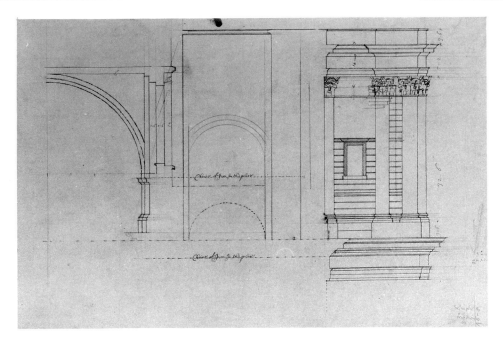

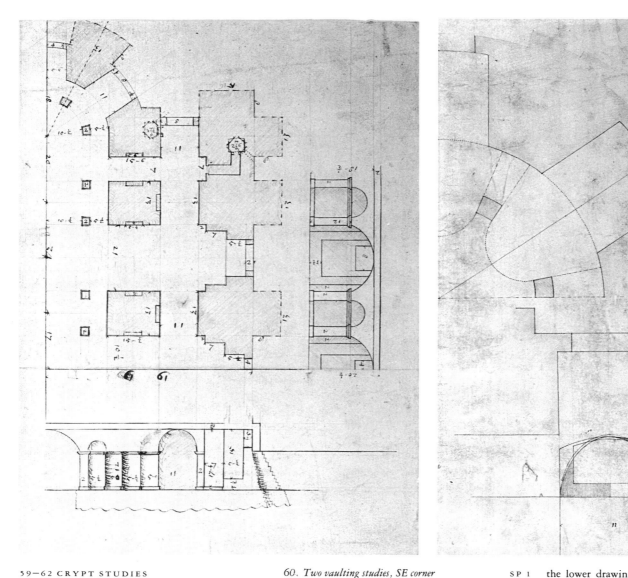

59—62 CRYPT STUDIES

59. Quarter-plan and sections of choir crypt   S P 2
356 x 257   Scale c.12ft
WS II/I top R (wrongly captioned)
Pen & pencil
Schematic drawing, cut at top (E). Not as built.

60. Two vaulting studies, SE corner   S P 1
405 x 246   Scale 4ft
WS II/I top L
Pencil, pen & wash
Early attempts to establish the geometry of apertures. The piers are shown as divided bases for the coupled pilasters above. The upper drawing is a plan of the S half of the apse, with section of the SE window vault; the lower drawing is a plan of the E wall of the S aisle, with section of the E end window. A note gives heights above the base lines of the section drawings, which is the top of the impost (or springing) of the crypt vaulting. This datum line was used in contracts and accounts for measurement of work, and corresponds externally to the division between the first and second courses of the ground level plinth.

61. *Plan and section of one aisle window*   SP 3
380 x 230   Scale c.4ft
WS II/I lower (wrongly captioned)
Pen & pencil
Inscribed: *Plan of a window in ye Cellar (6).* This is
possibly in Hawksmoor's hand and, if so, may relate
to re-use of an early drawing in the 1690s. Like No.
60 the base level is the vault impost.

62. *Duplicate of No. 61*   BUTE 17
525 x 369   Scale c.4ft
Pen & pencil

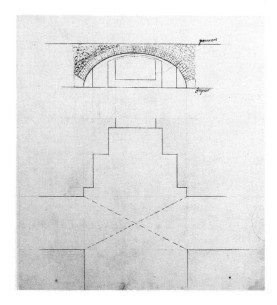

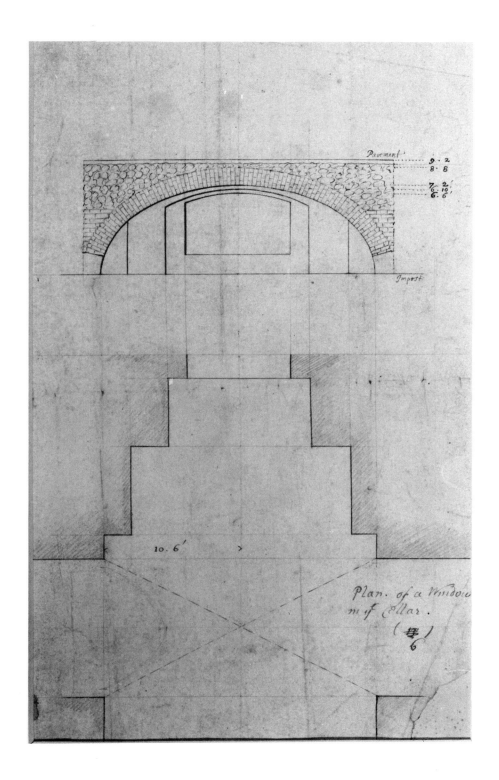

Categorising the St Paul's drawings by scale reveals, among others, a group which is coherent and which comprises almost all the drawings to 10ft scale. These are part-plans, part-elevations and part-sections of the E end, transept/crossing, and W end. Their significance has been overlooked partly because six of the ten, including two very faint pencil drawings, were not reproduced in WS. They are in fact models of economy: with hardly any duplication of information, they provide enough material for any draughtsman, once told the number of bays, to draw out the whole design, inside and outside, except the dome and towers. No drawing traverses either of the main axes of the church, and apart from these axes half-windows are shown; this method of division corresponds to that used for the allocation of building contracts at St Paul's.

In details the design shown is consistently a revision of the Definitive: the Composite orders are reinstated, the transept end window architraves are like those in the fabric, rustication is shown throughout, and the external base plinth is of two courses of masonry as executed. This feature does not appear with consistency in any previous group.

63. *Plan of NE corner of choir*   SP 6
308 x 229   Scale 10ft
Pen
Differs in some details from the fabric.

64. *N half of E elevation*   SP 22
355 x 250   Scale c. 10ft
Pencil & pen
As built except in small details of window sills and architraves.

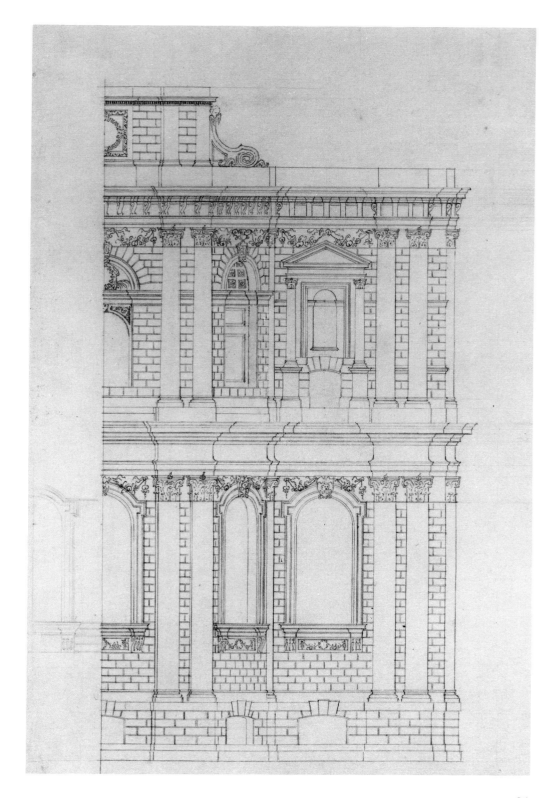

65. *E end of N elevation*
347 x 216   Scale c.10ft
WS II/IX
Pencil & pen
Agrees with No. 64.

66. *E–W section of E end*   SP 61
359 x 229   Scale c.10ft
WS XIII/IV
Pencil & pen
As built except for minor details of panelling.

67. *Plan of half transept and quarter of crossing*   S P 8
332 x 483   Scale c. 10ft
WS II/V upper
Pencil & pen
Not entirely as built: the great stair to the dome was
not built in this quarter, and the aisle windows were
made less nearly semicircular in plan.

68. *Half transept end, bastion and half aisle bay*   S P 2 1
357 x 470   Scale c. 10ft
Pencil
The pilaster flanking the transept window has a reveal
and its capital a cherub-head, as in the fabric; the
window architrave is near to its present form. Candelabra are shown on the corner parapet of the
transept. Too faint to reproduce.

94

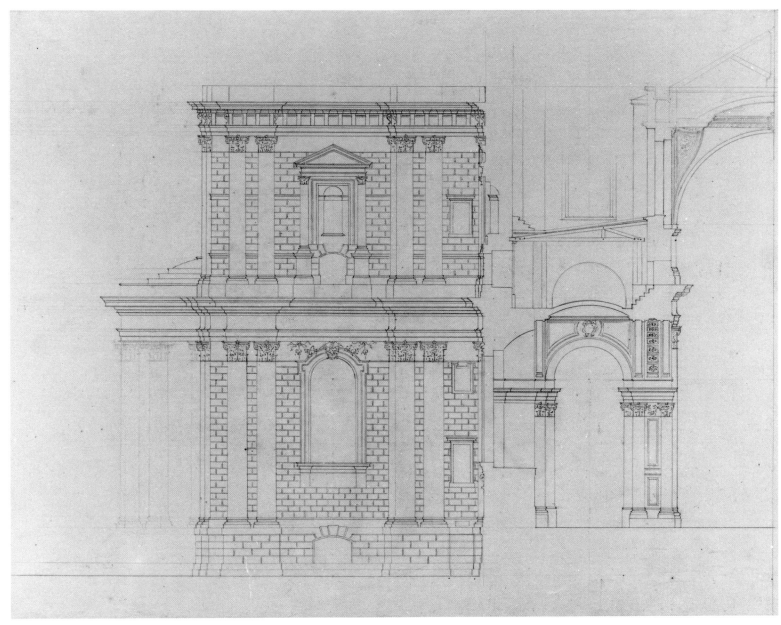

69. *Side elevation of portico and transept, with half-section*
of nave   S P 2 4
335 x 452   Scale c.10ft
Pencil & pen

70. *Plans of NW and SW quarters*   SP 5
515 x 585   Scale c.10ft
WS II/III upper (NW quarter only)
Pen

There are many small dimensional differences between the two quarters, which are drawn separately
on one sheet. The NW, in outline, is closer to the
elevation No. 71; the SW, which is hatched, is closer
to the fabric, being slightly wider and having a wider
centre bay in the portico.

71. *N half of W elevation*   SP 20
470 x 350   Scale c.10ft
Pencil
Shows aedicules and triforium-level windows in the
upper storey of the towers; the fabric has pedimented
windows with panels beneath them.

72. Half-bay of nave and elevation of NW chapel and tower   SP 25
341 x 456   Scale c.10ft
Pencil & pen
As No. 71, shows aedicules and windows in the upper
storey of the towers and above the chapels.

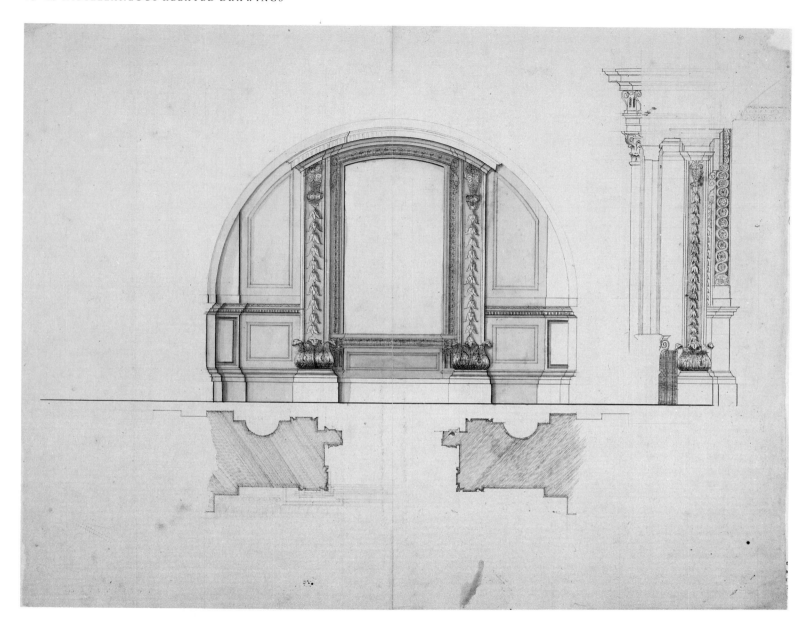

73. *Interior study for transept window*   BUTE 10
466 x 597   Scale 4ft
Pencil, pen & grey wash
Superseding No. 46, but further modified in detail in
execution during the 1690s.

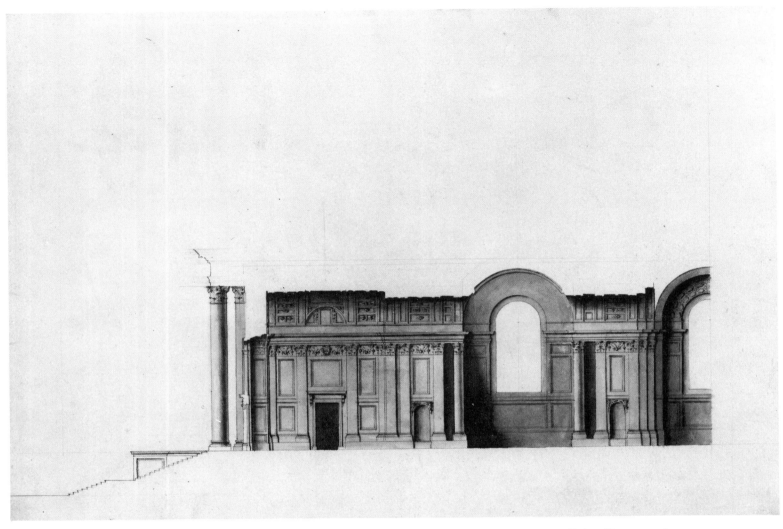

74. *W–E section, W end of N aisle*　　　　SP 65
330 x 485　Scale c.10ft
WS II/XI lower
Pen & grey wash
A fine drawing, close to the fabric; possibly related to
the 10ft set (Nos. 70–72), but the use of wash
suggests a drawing intended for engraving in 1702.

75. *Half-plan of S transept end*　　　　SP 7
483 x 350　Scale c.5ft
WS II/VI upper
Pen & black ink & black & red chalk
Fairly close to the fabric but the crypt window splays
(in red) do not conform.

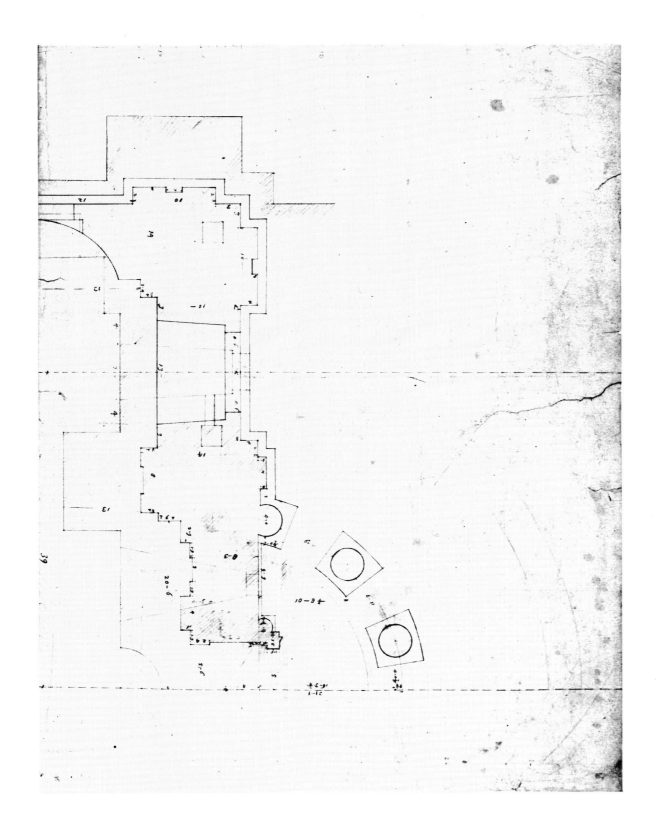

101

76. *E–W section of E end* SP 120
494 x 626   Scale 5ft
Pencil & pen
Unfinished; cut L and R. Close to the fabric.

77. *W–E section, three bays of nave and dome pier* S P 5 8
527 x 686   Scale 5ft
WS II/XX
Pen & grey wash
Mostly as built, but the archivolt nearest the crossing
was left plain.

78. *W–E section through portico and W bays*   S P 60
356 x 450   Scale c.9½ft
WS XIII/XXII
Pencil & pen
A later stage than No. 52; Composite small order and
upper outer order.

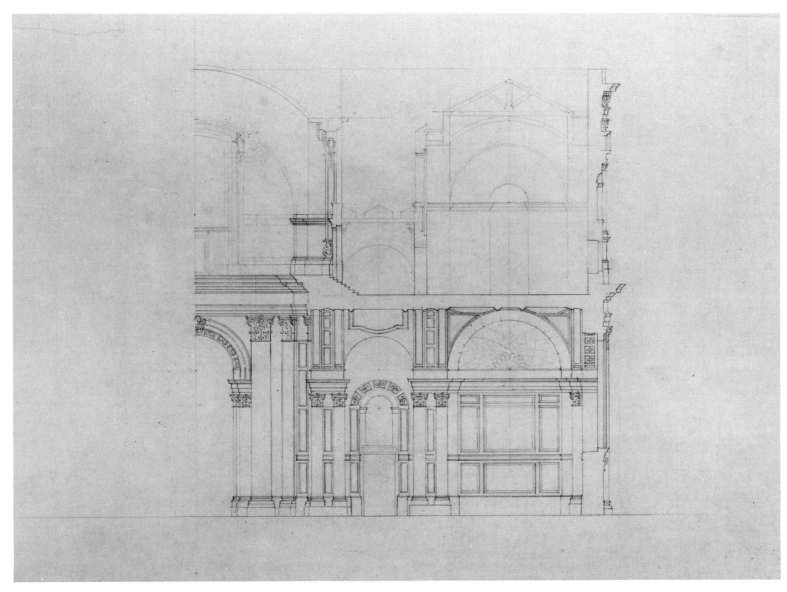

79. *Half-section through nave and NW chapel*   SP 62
332 x 430   Scale c.9½ft
WS XIII/XXIII
Pencil & pen
Most of the upper storey in pencil. The N side of the
Trophy Room still has a screen-wall aedicule instead
of a window.

80. *Revision of upper half of No. 79*   S P 6 9
326 x 423   Scale c.6ft
WS XIII/XXIV
Pen & pencil
The aedicule in the N wall has been replaced by a
window similar in profile to the fabric.

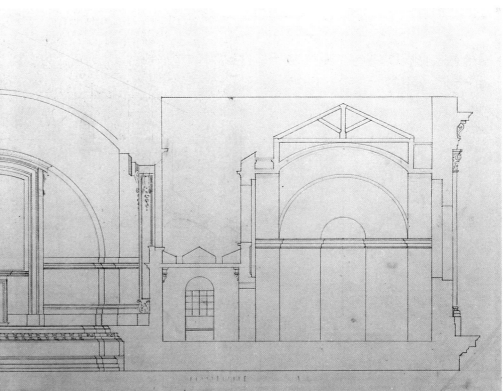

81. *W–E section through NW tower and Trophy Room*
                   S P 7 1

322 x 481   Scale 7ft
WS II/XXII lower
Pen & pencil
Inscribed in pencil: *This Side 2*
Cut L. Suggesting a belfry, below the main parapet,
with apertures between the brackets of the Composite
frieze. A great bell is indicated in pencil.

82. *E–W section through Library and SW tower*
                   S P 1 2 5 A

279 x 365   Scale 7ft
WS XIII/XXV upper
Pen & grey wash
Corresponds to No. 81 in reverse.

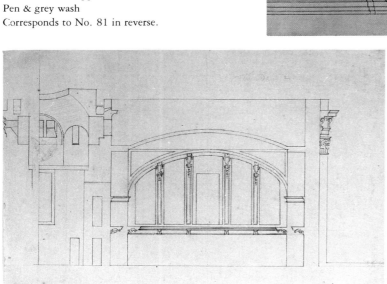

83. *Half E–W section of Library* SP 72
451 x 297   Scale 7ft
Pen
Corresponds to part of No. 82.

84. *S–N section through Library and W dome* SP 125B
314 x 414   Scale 7ft
WS XIII/XXV lower
Pen
Corresponds in reverse to No. 80.

85. *E–W section through Library or Trophy Room*
BUTE 14
362 x 470   Scale 6ft
Pen & pencil
Tower marked in pencil on R. Two halves showing alternative proposals for vaulting.

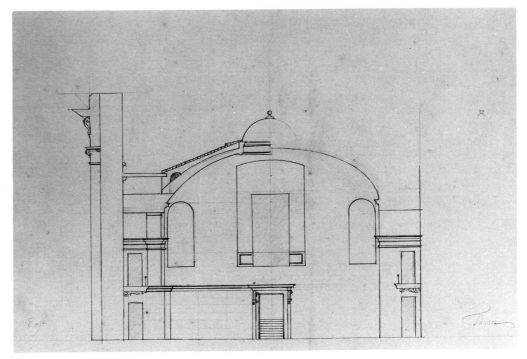

St Paul's dome was Wren's obsession from the time of his Pre-fire report and drawings presented respectively in May and August 1666, after his return from Paris. In profile and in several significant levels the final design made after 1700 is remarkably close to those first drawings, but the concept passed through large excursions in the intervening 35 years. Not only were the shape and the statical system subject to many changes, but also the number of bays into which the peristyle was divided. This ranged from 16, as in the Penultimate and Definitive drawings, through 24 (a return to the Pre-fire project) to 32 as in the fabric; all these were considered during 1675 around the time of the Definitive design, as well as a design with a drum of eight concave sides. It appears that, having explored a number of options and satisfied himself that they could be supported by the structure beneath, Wren left the form of the dome in abeyance until about 1697, when the choir was completed and opened and financial as much as structural support was a matter for concern. In February 1700 he brought, at the Commission's order, a complete design for the building; this was presumably the basis of the authorized engravings of 1702 which show the exterior up to the peristyle in accordance with the fabric (see No. 205). There are no dome studies for which a date can be established during the intervening quarter-century.

86. Study for a dome on an octagonal drum   SP 168B
260 × 302   Scale 20ft
WS XIII/III upper
Pen & pencil
WS XII, p.203, suggested that this design was connected with the First Model of 1669–70, which had a domed W vestibule. This impressionistic idea cannot be sustained. Assuming a scale of 20ft as in most of the other studies, the total span is appropriate for the Penultimate and the pedimented porticoes accord with the width of the nave and transepts. Diagonal drum windows also fit the Penultimate, but this design would certainly look large above a building without screen walls: the height from the roof-line (indicated on the R) to the base of the lantern would be almost that of the present outer dome, or about 40ft higher than in the Penultimate. On the other hand this design would be compatible with the introduction of screen walls, and the parallelism between the drum porticoes and the pedimented transept ends would not necessarily have worried Wren.

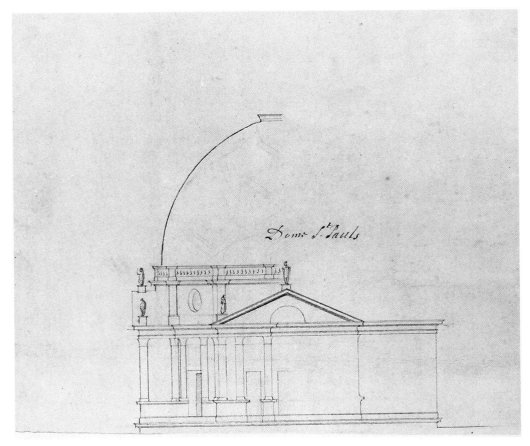

87. Study for a dome of 16 sides　　　　SP 163
432 x 349　Scale 20ft
WS III/XXV R
Pen & pencil
In the lowest drum rectangular windows are pencilled beneath the oval frames of the stage above. This design would fit the Penultimate, which has sixteen sides and has similar oval windows (but twice as many) at the bottom of the cupola.

88. Comparative sections of Nos. 87 and 89　　SP 112A
435 x 301　Scale 20ft
WS III/XXX L (as SP 172)
Pen & pencil
Establishes the proximity of these two designs, and shows the first known introduction of a cone above the inner dome; this idea is of the essence of Wren's final solution.

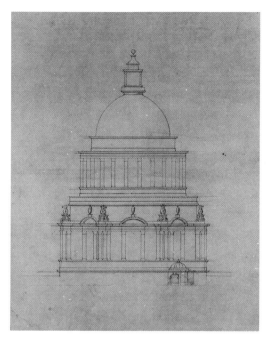

89. Elevation of dome on a concave octagonal podium

SP 167

431 x 317   Scale 20ft
WS III/XXVIII R
Pen & pencil

In true elevation this design is not easy to read, but it will be found to fit Nos. 88 and 90. It also shares flaming pinnacles with the former and the little domed exedrae over the quarter-galleries with the latter. The segmental pediments, omitted from the perspective, No. 90, occur alternately in the centres and at the junctions of the eight faces of the podium.

90. Perspective of dome with a concave octagonal podium

SP 172

459 x 340   Based on a scale of 20ft
WS III/XXX R
Pen & pencil
Part of the plan appears on No. 93. Some of the construction lines for the perspective can be seen on No. 91. The early dating of this design has added significance in that Wren is not usually supposed to have developed an interest in the Borrominesque play of concave and convex before his more "Baroque" phase in the 1690s. The answer indeed may be that his source was Guarini's unexecuted dome for Ste Anne-la-Royale in Paris; Wren surely met Guarini there as an expert on domes, in 1665. This drawing and the lost original of No. 94 are among the very few perspectives attributable to Wren, whose expressed emphasis on an architect's skill in perspective was a matter of mental rather than manual accomplishment.

91. Studies related to No. 90

SP 166

454 x 352   Scale 20ft
WS III/XXVIII L
Pen & pencil
Top R, faint pencil plan of an unidentified structure. Lower, L, half cross-section of the crossing beneath half-elevation of the podium of no. 90 with pencil outline of the dome of the same. The drum immediately above the podium is divided into bays by pier-strips and relief panels and surmounted by a balustrade. To the R, diagonal half-section through the crossing (including bastion corner staircase) beneath section of a different dome and drum, fairly close to No. 99. Part plans of both these appear on No. 93.
Verso: black pen plan and elevation of a two-stage lantern with diagonal buttresses, on a platform bounded by a metal railing. Careful but somewhat naive drawing, of no ascertainable connection with St Paul's.

314 x 193   Scale 26ft

WS III/XXVII R

Pen

Top R, a word which appears to be *Quid*. L of the drawing, upside down, a calculation dividing 108 by 7. The internal diameter is 108ft, but why it should be divided by 7 is a puzzle: a mathematician wishing to obtain the circumference by π ($^{22}/_7$) would probably multiply before dividing. The drawing shows (L) half cross-section and (R) half diagonal elevation and (below) quarter-plan; since it is free-hand, correspondences are approximate, but there is a scale of divisions of 10ft at the top of the plan. The projecting lobes are to be understood from the plan as standing above the quarter-galleries; hence the reading of the elevation as diagonal. However, the roof-line of the church below is not rendered with consistency, and at the extreme L of the section there appears the profile of a diagonal lobe. Yet perhaps consistency should not be expected in a sketch of this kind which records an otherwise unknown solution. The difference in height between the inner and outer windows is as complex as in any design for the dome.

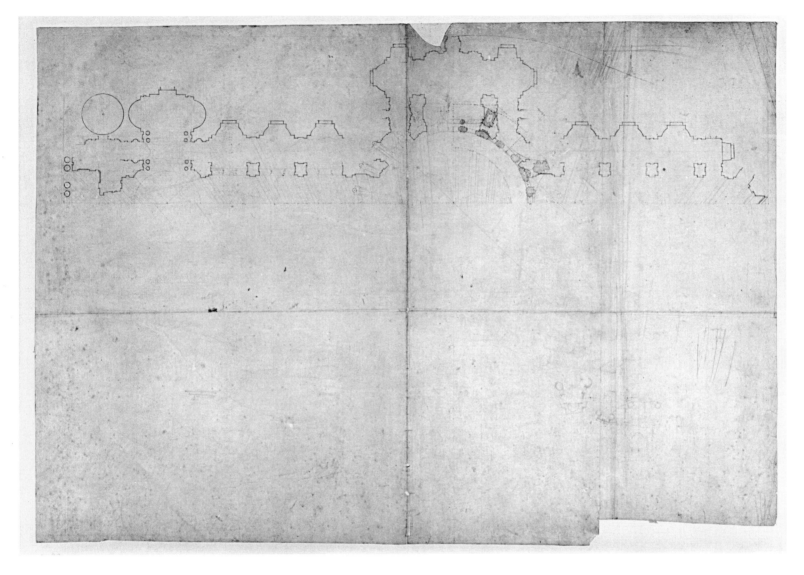

93. *Half internal plan with eighths of four domes*   S P 9 1
504 x 688   Scale 20ft
Pencil & pen
N half plan showing only internal surfaces; probably
made specifically in connection with the perspective
long section of which an engraving was paid for in
April 1703 and of which No. 94 is an early proof. The
engraving is in reverse sense. On No. 93 construction
lines can be seen converging to a point on the transept
axis near the bottom (S) edge of the drawing; these
relate to the perspective parts of the engraving. The
bottom R (SE) quarter of the sheet has two faint
pencil sketches of pier masses similar to those in the

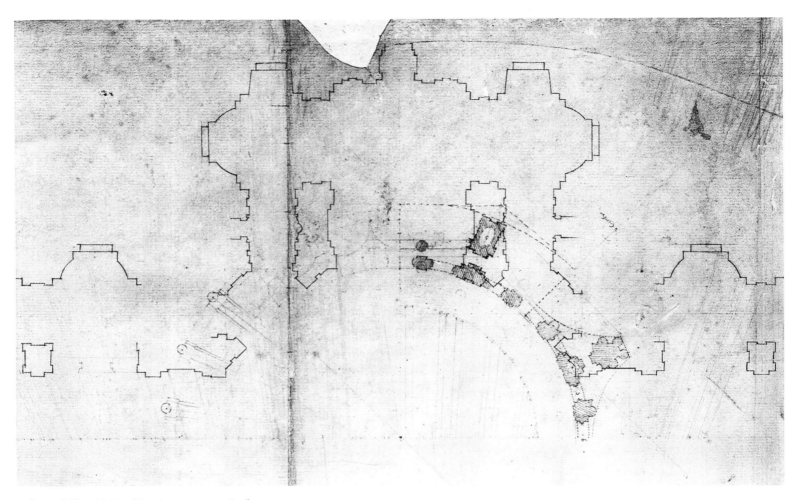

podium of Nos. 90–91. More important are the four eighth-plans of domes superimposed on the main drawing. Going clockwise from W to E these are of the designs Nos. 97, 99, 89–90 and 91. Together with the pencil sketches and the close relationship to No. 94, the presence of these alternatives on one sheet helps to establish the chronological proximity and early date of three different solutions – four if No. 91 is considered as distinct.

114

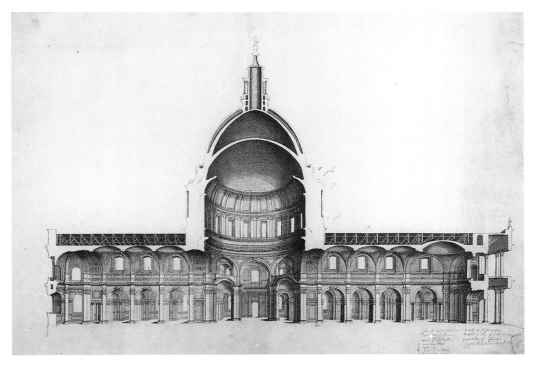

94. Proof engraving of E–W section. Definitive design

SP 119 is a print of the final state, titled *Section of the Cathedral Church of St Paul Lond. Wherein the Dome is represented according to a Former Design of the Architect Sr CHR. WREN Kt.* It is similarly titled in Latin. This proof copy lacks all letters, the scale, and anything more than the outlines of the section across the peristyle. A series of pen notes at bottom R instructs the engraver to make various amendments and remove blemishes, and alternative moulding profiles are drawn L and R of the peristyle section. The profiles and notes are possibly in Hawksmoor's hand; some of them may not have been Wren's intention and the profiles were not altered. The most significant alteration made was the subject of the first note, *Cover the first faces all over very faint*; that is the light hatching of pilasters, piers and attic.

The engraving and the corrections date from 1702–03, but the design, *Juxta priorem sententiam*, is clearly intended to be seen as earlier and superseded; the question is how much earlier. Other authorized engravings of 1702–03, probably based on older drawings, were updated in the process; this one by contrast was intended to be of historical interest. Both in the upper columns of the W portico and in the small internal order Corinthian capitals are shown, as has been mentioned in the preface to No. 11. Thus the engraver used a drawing made no later than 1675.

Wren must have wished to record this design of dome because it pleased him. It is similar, though not identical, to the section in No. 95, and broadly in conformity with the All Souls elevation (Fig XIV); it is not one of the solutions shown on the plan No. 93. See also No. 95.

96. Variant of No. 95, part elevation and plan SP 168A
249 x 358   Scale 20ft
WS XIII/III lower
Pencil, pen & grey wash
Only the hemisphere is shown; it ends at the bottom with a ruled line fractionally above the edge of the paper. Pencilled grids below and R of the outline plan probably represent roof trusses.

95. *Section/elevation and half-plan of dome, Definitive design*   SP 171
468 x 305   Scale 20ft
WS III/XXIX R
Pen & pencil

Made up of four pieces of paper pasted to a base sheet, which bears a number of ruled lines suggesting a page layout; the pencil sketches on the reverse of this sheet thus may or may not relate to the peristyle. The largest pasted-on piece contains the half-section of the dome, and below it a quarter plan at peristyle level (marked A) and eighth plans at attic window level (B) and at the springing of the outer dome (C). The outer dome and drum elevations are on two separate pieces, and the lantern is another piece cut out round the outline. Nevertheless all the drawing is from one hand, and that undoubtedly Woodroffe's.

The drawing shares with No. 94 and the All Souls S elevation (Fig.00) the peculiarity of a design of 16 bays with piers on the axes rather than, as is the case in all other St Paul's designs, bay centres on the axes. This peculiarity is also found in the Dome of the Invalides in Paris, where the drum is dodecagonal; however, the foundation of this church by Jules Hardouin Mansart was not laid until 1677 and it would be foolish to suppose either that Wren had foreknowledge of the design or that his own design must be later. Such a methodological dilemma is obviated, although not to the point of certainty, by reference to the surviving sketches by François Mansart for a Bourbon mausoleum at Saint-Denis, one of which (A. Braham and P. Smith, *François Mansart*, London, 1973, Pl. 457) shows a section of a dodecagonal dome of this kind. Iconographically the Dome of the Invalides was the successor to the Saint-Denis project, for which the sketches were made and under discussion during the summer of 1665; Wren on his way to Paris was expecting to meet the elder Mansart early in July 1665. In these circumstances it is possible that a Bourbon drawing was also a common source for the rim at the base of both the Invalides dome and that in No. 95 which hides from below a ring of attic windows which light the inner dome.

Three other features are noteworthy in No. 95: (1) The oval windows around the base, similar in shape and size to those in the Penultimate and in Nos. 87–88, but here lighting only the external gallery under the peristyle. (2) An indication in the section of the inner dome of figures, showing that an illusionist cupola painting was considered: Pierre Mignard's decoration of the dome of the Val-de-Grâce in Paris was nearing completion while Wren was there. (3) A series of straight lines converging downwards in the L quarter of the plan: these suggest that this drawing was used for the perspective of the dome in No. 94.

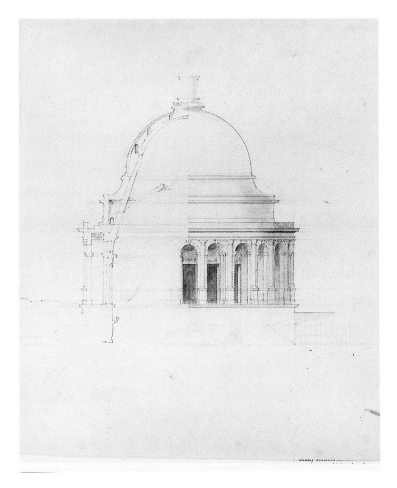

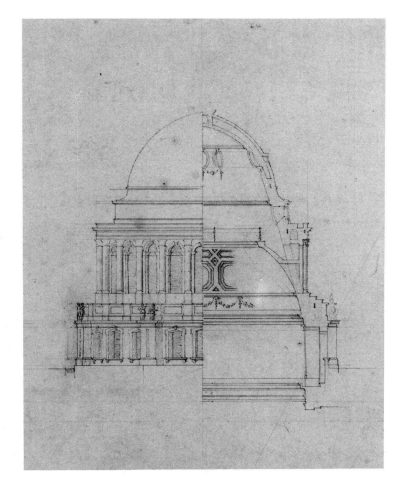

97. *Half elevation/section of 24-sided dome*   SP 164
403 x 325
WS III/XXVI R
Pen, pencil & grey wash
Bottom L, rough pencil plan of a quarter of peristyle.
One eighth plan appears on No. 93, confirming an
early date.

98. *Half-elevation/section of 24-sided dome*   SP 161
483 x 353
WS III/XXV L
Pen & pencil
Faint L quarter-plan below in pencil. The drum below
the peristyle is divided into segments by eight projecting piers. The inside and outside domes are hard
to relate to each other in respect of fenestration.
Verso: in reverse aspect, pencil part-section of a dome
similar to Nos. 100–101, with which it is discussed.

99. *Half section/elevation of 24-sided dome with concave drum faces* SP 165A

381 x 230 Scale 20ft

WS III/XXVII L

Pen & pencil

Top L, pencil sketch of part of a peristyle. Bottom L, one eighth plan showing a semicircular recess between each of the peristyle columns. This corresponds to one segment of No. 93.

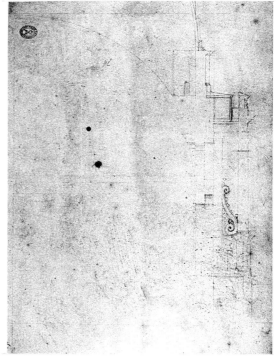

118

100. *Half section/elevation of 32-sided dome*   S P 1 6 2
476 x 331   Scale 20ft
WS III/XXVI L
Pen & grey wash

Wren's final solution was a dome with a peristyle of
32 bays, every fourth intercolumniation being filled
to form a pier mass. This number of bays had already
appeared in the Greek Cross and Great Model designs, and the change to sixteen in the Penultimate
marks a change of scale. Thereafter he considered
several alternatives, and this scheme for 32 bays is
certainly of 1675. It retains the diagonal windows at
the base of the drum, though they only light a
passage; also the drum itself is still octagonal in plan.
The elevation, but not the section, shows huge
brackets placed radially inside the columns of the
peristyle; this combination is drawn out in section on
a larger scale (6ft) on the reverse of No. 98. It may
further be noted that in both drawings, as in No. 101
which is a variant without the brackets, the inside of
the peristyle is cylindrical and not conical as was
finally decided by 1698.

The reverse has a few indecipherable pencil marks.

101. *Part section similar to No. 100*   S P 1 7 0
526 x 370   Scale 6ft
WS III/XXIX L
Pencil, pen & grey wash
Cut on all sides.

This is a topographical grouping, for convenience, of studies which it is impossible to date narrowly. One quarter of the crossing was of the essence, visually and structurally, of designs from the Pre-fire project onwards, and naturally Wren made detailed studies of the area at various levels. Probably all these drawings were made early; five show the spiral staircase in the corner bastion not as in the fabric. However, Nos. 106 and 108 have superimposed plans of the dome at a much later stage, and must be either resuscitations or copies of earlier drawings.

102. Quarter plan of crossing and transept   SP 95
605 x 417   Scale c.6ft
WS III/I lower
Pen & red chalk
Chalk is used for a superimposed plan at triforium level. The crossing is here considered merely as an octagon. Before it was cut on all sides this plan covered the same area as No. 67 and, without the hatching, is identical in draughtsmanship.

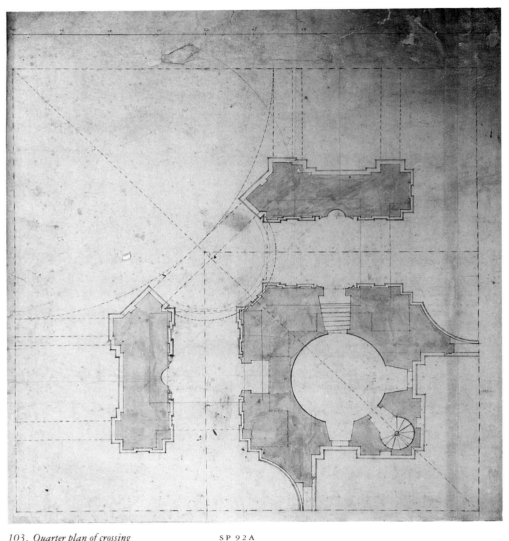

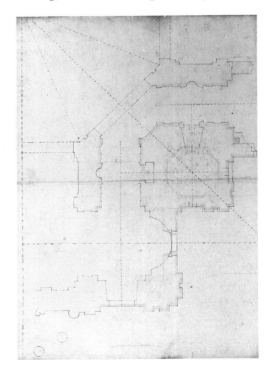

103. Quarter plan of crossing   SP 92A
482 x 444   Scale 6ft
WS III/I upper L
Pen, grey wash & red chalk
Chalk is used for the outlines of walls at a higher level which cannot be related to other surviving drawings.

120

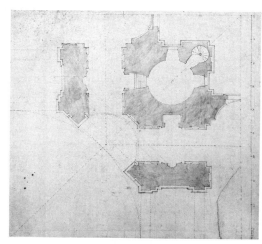

104. *Version of No. 103* SP 93
477 x 428   Scale c.6ft
Pen, pencil & grey wash
Differs from No. 103 in the absence of chalk lines and
in the rendering of thicknesses and profiles.

105. *Quarter plan of crossing, eighth plan of peristyle*
SP 12
365 x 475   Scale c.6ft
WS II/V lower
Pen
Same hand as No. 104. The peristyle is of 32 bays
with pier masses in every fourth bay. The semi-
circular staircase shafts are in the outer halves of these
piers, as in the fabric (and not as in No. 108). But the
interior circumference of the peristyle passes through
the corners of the basic crossing octagon rather than
through its sides; this implies a wider peristyle than
in the fabric and therefore one which is cylindrical
rather than conical, as in No. 101 which is compatible with this plan.

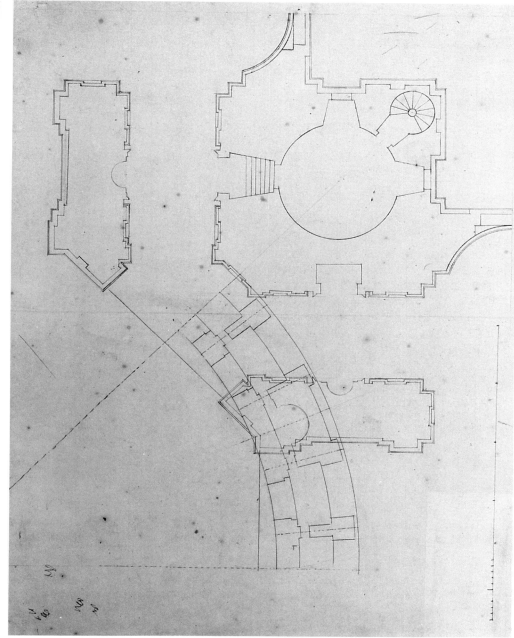

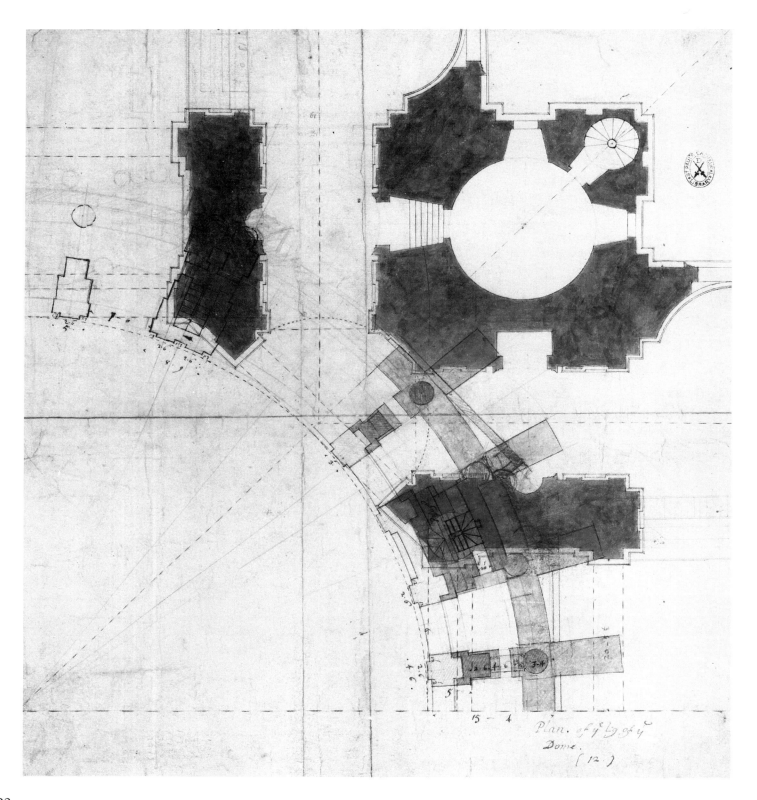

Plan. of y.^e b.^y of y.^e
Dome.

(12)

122

106. Quarter plan of crossing with ideas for peristyle

SP 11

471 x 447   Scale c.6ft

WS II/IV

Pencil, black pen, blue, yellow & grey wash & black
& red chalk

This drawing has the same provisional rendering of
the spiral stair as others in this group. The peristyle
plans, with the inscription *Plan, of ye leg of ye Dome
(12)*, were probably added towards the end of the
century. One segment shows a confused arrangement,
partly in black chalk, of piers and columns, in which
can be seen in red chalk half of a concave section
similar to No. 90. The other segment shows part of a
peristyle very close to the fabric, with the radial
buttresses outside the Whispering Gallery that are a
characteristic feature of the final design: these are
washed in blue and yellow.

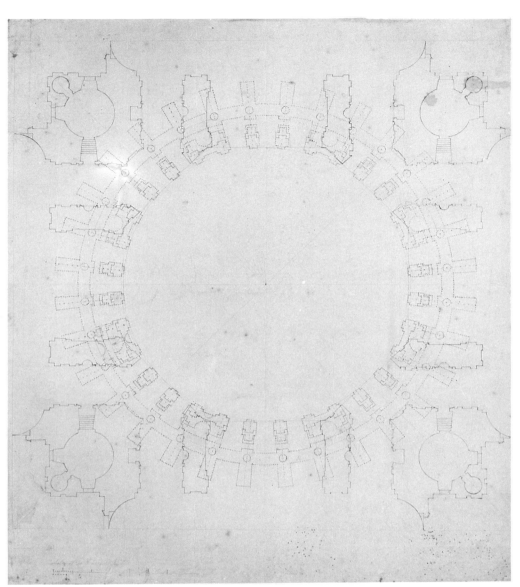

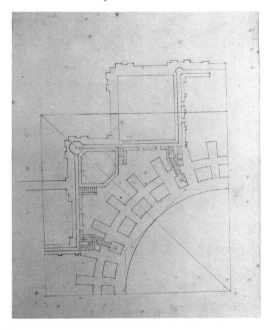

107. *Quarter plan of crossing at drum level*   SP 15

365 x 476   Scale 9ft

WS II/III lower

Pen

As executed.

108. *Schematic plan of crossing, drum and peristyle* SP 13

581 x 507   Scale c.10ft

WS XIII/XII

Pen

The four bastions are shown as identical: this must
mean a mechanical repetition of one quarter without
regard to the specification of vestries and great
staircase. On this scheme is superimposed a plan of
several levels of the conical peristyle finally built,
except that the filled pier masses have the stair shafts
inwards (Cf. No. 105 which agrees with the fabric).

123

109. *Half plan and section of NW (Lord Mayor's) Vestry*

BUTE 16

458 x 297   Scale 2ft
Pencil & pen
Schematic, without the vault, enriched mouldings or joinery.

110. *Part plan of SE (Dean's) Vestry*   BUTE 15

345 x 332   Scale 2ft
Pen
The top is torn off obliquely.

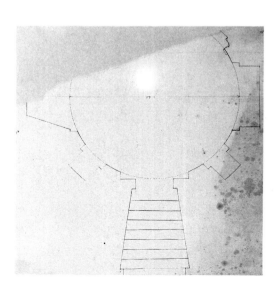

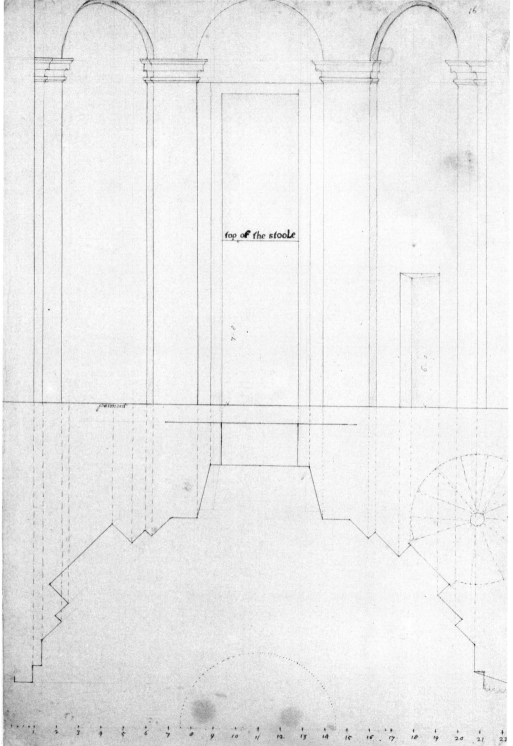

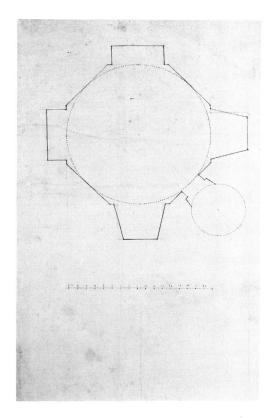

111. Plan and section of SE (Dean's) Vestry SP 123A
366 x 253 Scale c.6ft
WS III/VIII L
Pen
The section shows two rooms superimposed; the lower represents the vestry, the higher and wider one is the chamber above it.

112 Outline plan of No. 111 SP 123B
413 x 255 Scale c.3ft
Pen

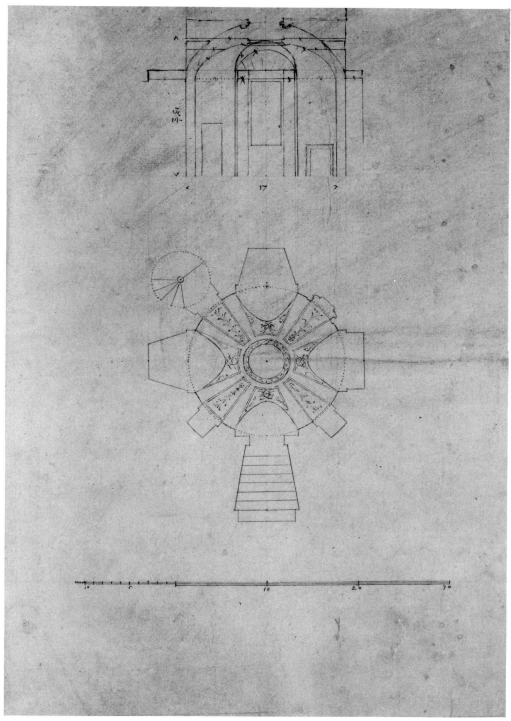

113. Plan and section of No. 111   SP 124
490 x 270   Scale c.3ft
WS III/VIII R
Pen & grey wash

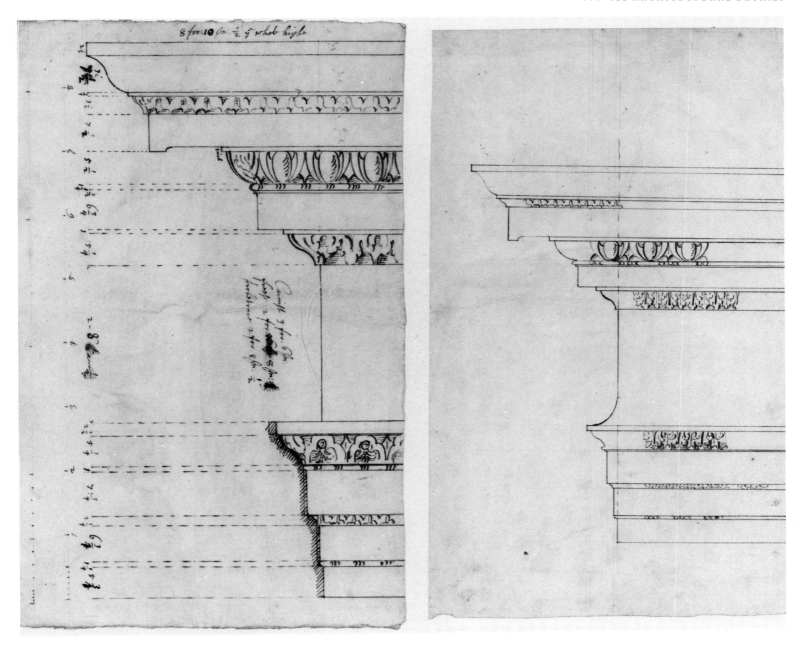

114. Two studies for main internal entablature   SP 138

(a) 428 x 264   Scale 1:7

(b) 415 x 260   Scale c.1:10

WS III/XIII upper

The L sheet is dimensioned, the R appears by a process of elimination to be an alternative to a smaller scale; neither is as executed. In particular the modilions are omitted from the cornice. The numerical dimensions in (a) are revisions of those drawn.

115. Details of interior main order

448 x 342   Scale 1:20

WS II/XXIII lower

Pen

Seven detail drawings, with a key in Roman numerals, nearly as executed. The precise setting out of the drawing, which is certainly in Wren's hand, may be compared with a sheet of details for Trinity College Library, Cambridge (now in the college: Whitechapel Art Gallery, *Sir Christopher Wren*, 1982, Fig. xvi) which must be of almost the same date. In No. 115 Wren has depicted plumb lines hanging from the cornices. The details shown are (I) main entablature; (II and III) bases of main and small pilasters; (IV and V) profile and face of main arcade archivolt; (VI and VII) small order entablature and the impost moulding above it.

116. Details of lower outside order

418 x 328   Scale 1:20

WS II/XV upper

Pen & pencil

Base and entablature, in Wren's hand and with the same conventions as No. 115. As executed.

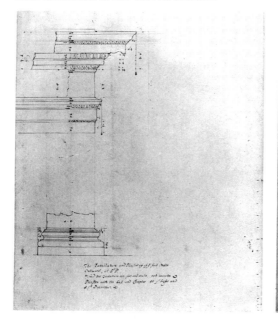

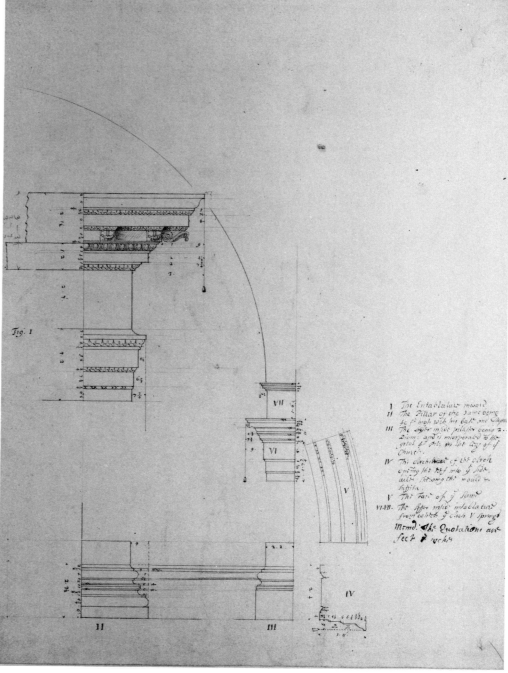

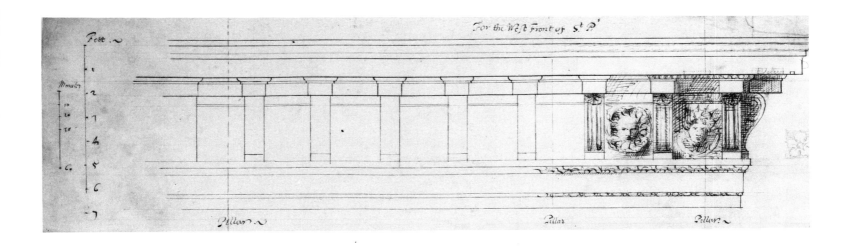

117. *Detail of upper outside entablature*   SP 46
144 x 490   Scale 1:20
WS II/XV lower
Pen & pencil
Trimmed. Corresponds in general to the fabric, including the setting of the consoles relative to column centres. But the executed detail of the consoles differs and the metopes were left plain all round the exterior. Inscribed *For the West Front of St P:s*. Not necessarily later than 1675.

118. *Details of internal attic*   SP 73
340 x 444   Scales c. 3ft and 1:4
WS II/XVI lower
Pen & pencil
Elevation of one bay, with masonry coursing ruled in pencil. Below, at 1:4 scale, profiles of the mouldings at top and bottom of the pedestal. Roughly as the fabric, but the clerestory window sill is higher than executed.

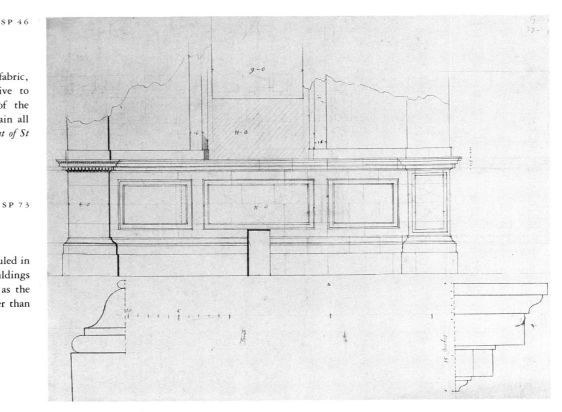

129

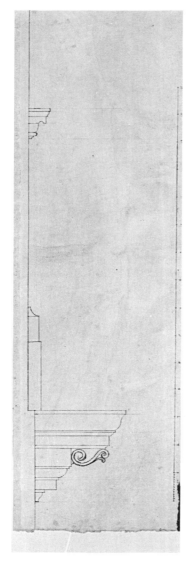

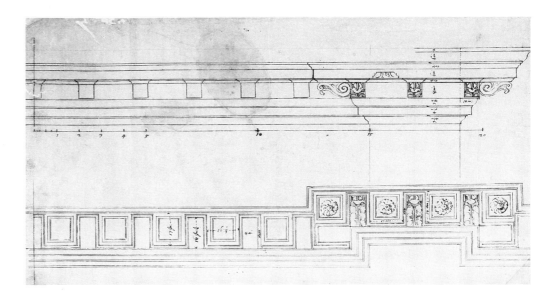

121. Plan and elevation of main internal cornice

SP 139C

290 x 526   Scale c.1ft
WS III/XIII bottom
Pen
Essentially as executed.

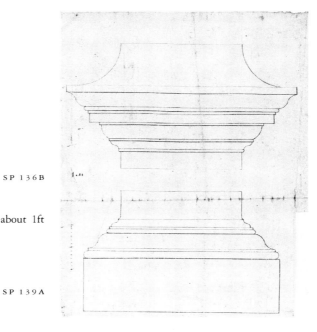

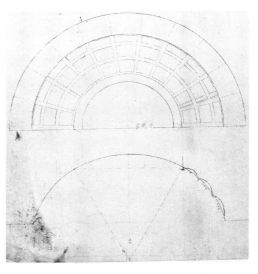

119. Profile of internal attic   SP 136B
535 x 216   Scale 1ft
Pen
Not as executed, the upper cornice being about 1ft
too low.

120. Top and base mouldings of internal attic   SP 139A
247 x 196   Scale 1:8
WS III/XIII centre L
Pen
Not as executed. The drawing has been mounted
upside down.

122. Setting out of coffering, transept aisle window   SP 74
362 x 452   Scale 2ft
WS II/XXIII upper
Pen & pencil
Endorsed: *ground plotts of the Concaves of the Windows at
St paules Church and the Eliptick Arch*. Elevation and
plan; the coffering pattern is that of the transepts. It
is possible to misread the elevation as "elliptical" (half
oval); in fact it is semi-circular and very slightly
stilted. Some very faint setting-out lines on the
reverse cannot be interpreted.

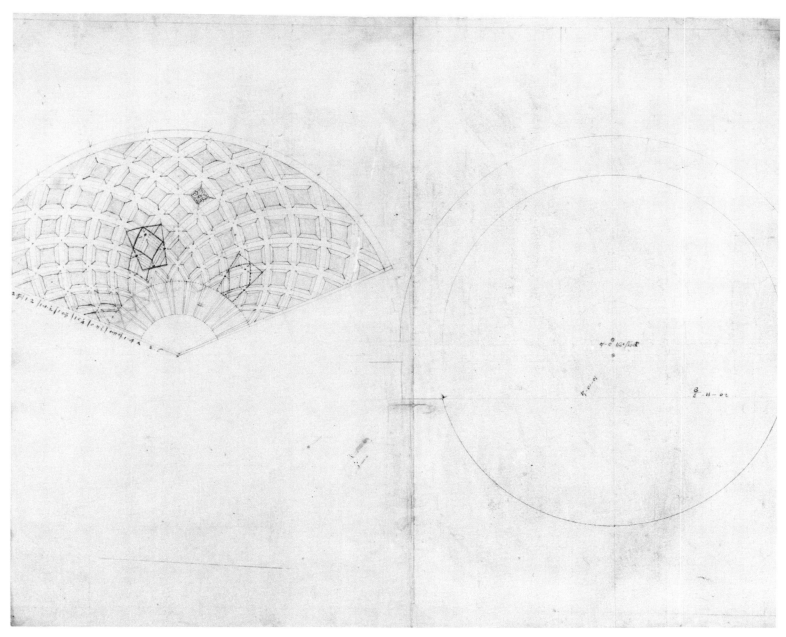

123. Setting out of coffering, W.chapel apses   S P 1 2 8
493 x 625   Scale 2ft
WS III/IV lower
Pen & pencil

On the reverse are several pencil diagrams. Taking the sheet in the same aspect, the two on the L are a plan and elevation of the inside of an aisle window, possibly belonging to the W chapels. The three on the R show the individual stones of window arches and indicate those which are "don" or "sett"; some are marked as ½in bigger than the mould, and the names of workmen are given including Remmington, Willis, Turner, Passmore, Rawlins, Wright, Powis, Farrist, Richards and Miller.

124. Study for transept outer doorcase   SP 43
410 x 253   Scale 1:32
Pen & pencil
Elevation and part plan, with pencil suggestion of overdoor panel and quarter-column flanking doorcase.

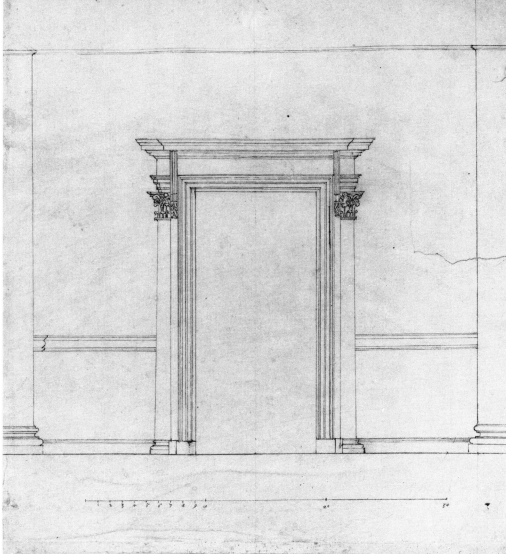

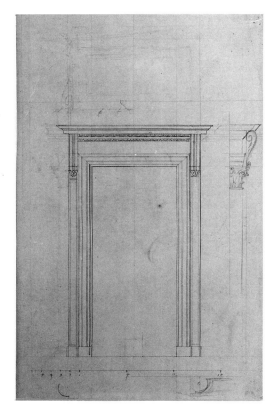

125. Revision of No. 124, elevation   SP 139B
319 x 278   Scale 4ft
WS III/XIII centre R
Pen
Elevation set in transept wall. Incorporates the quarter-columns sketched in the previous drawing.

126. Half-plan of No. 125   SP 92B
120 x 442   Scale 4ft
WS III/I upper R
Pen

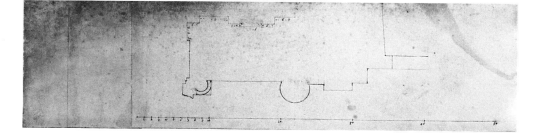

127. Further revision of No. 124   S P 4 2
445 x 274   Scale 1:32
Pen & pencil
With overdoor panel and part of frieze.

128. Further revision   S P 1 3 7
445 x 249   Scale c. 1:30
WS III/XII L
Pen, pencil & grey wash
Largely as executed. The relieving arch behind the
overdoor is indicated in pencil.

129. Further revision of overdoor decoration   SP177A
240 x 370   Scale c.1:30
WS III/XXXIII upper
Pen, pencil & grey wash

130. Plan of portico architrave   SP136A
538 x 268   Scale 2ft
Pen

Three bays out of five; the centre one is wider, as executed. *Verso:* pen drawing of the masonry coursing of the springing of two arches from a common pier.

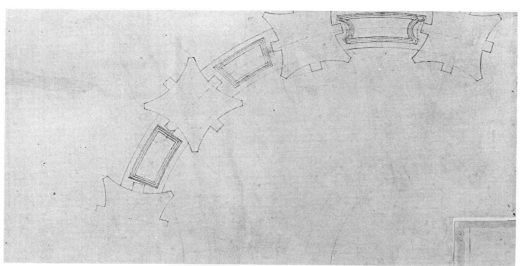

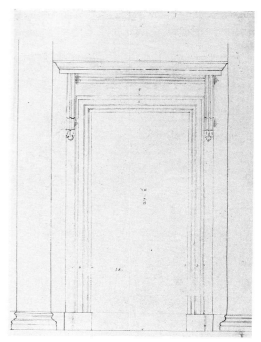

134

Probably all these are from the 1690s; only No. 133 can be approximately dated.

131. Elevation of W doorcase　　　SP 169B
381 x 280　Scale 3ft
WS XIII/XVIII bottom R (as SP 126)
Pen
Basically as executed, but without the moulding enrichments, and the flanking pilasters are too close.

132. Study W elevation with giant order portico　SP 140
476 x 624　Scale c. 10ft
WS III/XIV
Pen
Schematic drawing showing a giant Composite (?) order. The panel in the entablature was perhaps intended to carry an inscription. Complementary to No. 133; probably by Hawksmoor.

136

133. *Cross-section of giant order portico*   S P 141

500 x 387   Scale c. 10ft

WS III/XV upper

Pen, pencil & grey wash

Inscribed on panel over main door: *II F.M. HOC D. PAVLI. VETVS CAR II REG ANNO MDI ABSOL . . . GVIE . . . MO III.E MAR.II RR NC ARCHITEL C AB EQVITE CHRISTO WREN.* Parts are too faint to read or missing altogether. On the L, half N-S section; on the R, W-E section, The same design as No. 132 with the same ambiguity of type in both the giant order and the second storey capitals. The appearance of an upper Corinthian might suggest a very early date, but the reference to William and Mary precludes this. It might then be supposed that Hawksmoor, who joined the St. Paul's office in 1691, was amusing himself privately with this project; but No. 134 is not in his hand, and we know from *Parentalia* that Wren gave serious consideration to a giant portico.

No. 133 is most probably datable between Hawksmoor's arrival in 1691 and the death of Queen Mary at the end of 1694.

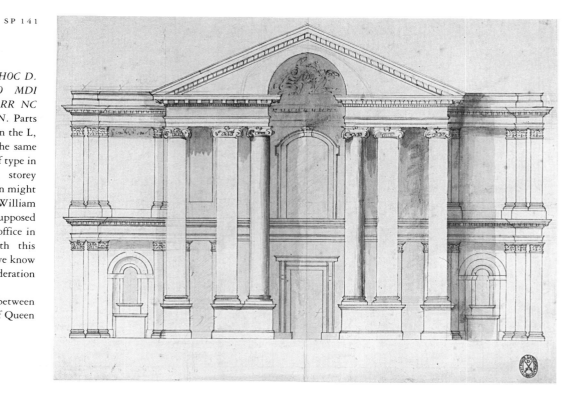

134. *Study W elevation with giant order portico*   S P 50

367 x 486   Scale c. 10ft

WS II/XVIII

Pen, pencil & grey wash

The basic elevation is poorly drawn. The tympanum relief seems to show two figures with a shield.

135. *Study W elevation with superimposed orders*

S P 143

355 x 490   Scale c. 10ft

WS III/XVII

Pen & grey wash

In pencil, belfries with corner urns, a much larger pediment and one giant column. Probably an adaption by Hawksmoor of another and very inaccurate elevation.

136. N elevation of W steps   SP 41

354 x 410   Scale 6ft

WS XIII/XVI lower R

Pen & pencil

Inscribed: *The north west corner of St. Paul's. The Steps are 14' and 5'.* This form of steps was determined by 1675 and appears in No. 15; it occurs also in the authorized engravings of 1702-03. The steps were finally built in 1709, Samuel Fulkes being paid for a mason's model "for the Great Flight of Steps at the W. End" in October 1708. The pyramidal form was then abandoned in favour of a widening flare with side rails down to the bottom step, as shown in Nos. 202 and 203. Wren was still in control of the building at this date and must have been responsible for the change. In 1872, after negotiations between the Chapter and the Corporation of London, The W end of the churchyard and the top of Ludgate Hill were re-arranged, and the W steps were rebuilt to the design of the Cathedral Surveyor, F. C. Penrose. Perhaps Penrose added to practical considerations the belief that he was restoring Wren's intentions (see also preface to No. 180); credit is at least due to him, without irony, for reverting to the engraved design rather than inventing his own.

137. N half of lower W wall of portico   SP 32

334 x 489   Scale c. 3ft

WS II/XIII upper

Pen & pencil

See No. 138.

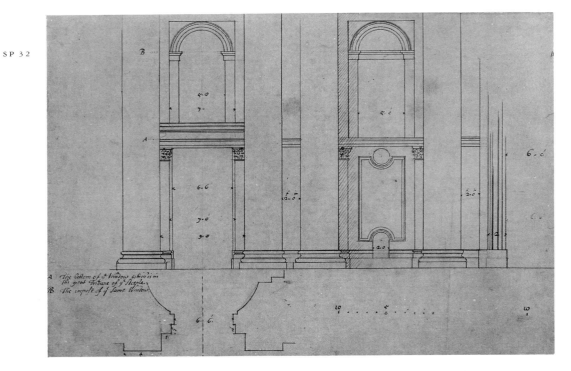

138

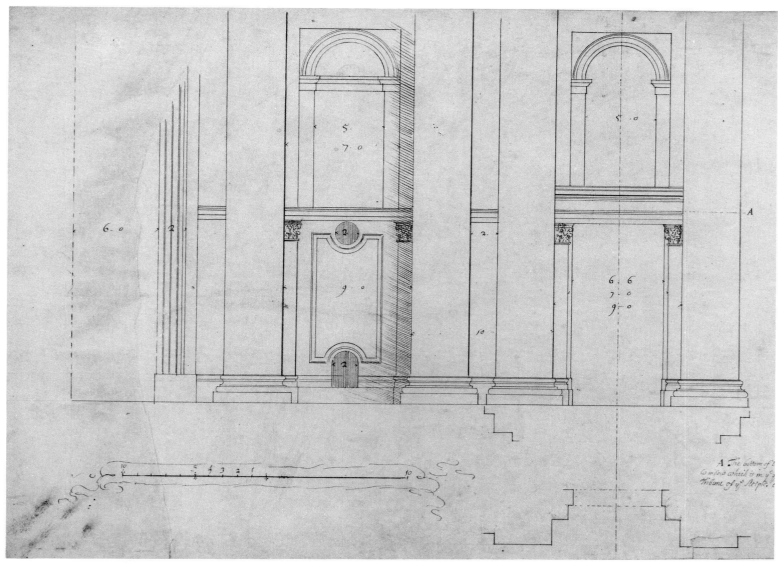

138. S half of lower W wall of portico   S P 1 3 5
360 x 486   Scale c. 3ft

WS XIII/XVII

Pen

Separate drawings which nevertheless belong
together. They are almost mirror images, and the
hatched shading runs in opposite directions, showing
that reverse hatching is not always the sign of a
left-handed draughtsman. The annotations, which
refer to the bottom tower windows, and the banner
round the scale in No. 138, are in Hawksmoor's
characteristic hand. Drawn in the early 1690s: the
middle pilasters are over a foot closer than in the
fabric.

The authorized prints of 1702-03 still show W towers of the cylindrical form, based on Bramante's Tempietto, that was designed in 1675 (Fig. 00). The towers had reached the cornice at the top of the church by 1701, and work was only resumed in 1705. Several drawings show the development of the 1675 towers to those of the 1702-03 prints, involving a general increase in height and the accommodation of a clock room and belfry. These drawings, mostly to a uniform but uncommon scale, are as much concerned with the structure and function of the towers as with their appearance, although in the process the number of columns in the peristyle went from 12 to 16. Finally the two sides of No. 154 show the imaginative leap to the more complex forms of the executed design. This sheet was discovered in 1951, and the recognition of Wren's hand in it by Sir John Summerson marked the turning point in the proper restitution of the final design to Wren, who had seemed to scholars for a generation previously a mind too staid to produce so exciting a design. See also commentary to No. 140.

139. *Plan of NW tower*   S P 1 4 8
293 x 246   Scale 10ft
WS III/XV lower
Pencil & pen
Inscribed: *AA is holes for weights.* This implies concern with the clock stage, which was ultimately situated in the SW tower. In some of the tower studies the clock and peal of bells are interchangeable from N to S and back. Probably drawn in the early 1690s since both giant and superimposed porticoes are indicated.

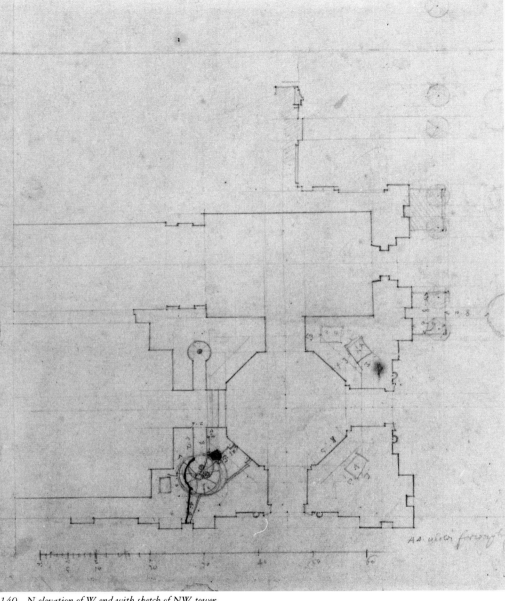

140. N elevation of W end with sketch of NW tower

S P 1 4 5

565 x 492   Scale c.6ft
WS III/XVIII L
Pen, pencil & grey wash
Made of two pieces joined 250 mm. from the top, probably in order to enlarge an older pen drawing when the wash sketch was added. The pen drawing is identical in scale and draughtsmanship to No. 16 and shows a Corinthian upper order; the wash sketch is quite different not only in style but in intention, being concerned with architectural members as wholes, as shapes and as images of light and shadow. Avray Tipping and Christopher Hussey in 1928 (*English Homes*, IV.ii,p.xviii) attributed the lower half to Hawksmoor and the upper to Vanbrugh. It is not now difficult to refute both suggestions, and it is on the other hand very probable that the lower half is by Wren or Woodroffe and the upper by Hawksmoor in consultation with Wren. Nos. 142-148 are developed from it.

142

141. Plan of NW tower

SP 149

385 x 500   Scale 10ft

Pencil

Inscribed top R *Scethes of ye West Steeple*: once used as a folder for other drawings, perhaps for this group. An otherwise unrecorded project with coupled columns placed diagonally across the corners of the clock stage.

142. Plan, elevation and half section of NW tower

SP 146

567 x 384   Scale c.5½ft

WS III/XIX L

Pen

In Hawksmoor's hand; his whimsical clock design denotes the passage of time by a winged hand. A free but disciplined drawing out of the idea in No. 140 with the concave corners of the clock stage unambiguously stated.

On the reverse, upside down, is a careful pen drawing of a fluted Doric column.

143. *Plan of SW tower similar to No. 142*   S P 1 5 1 A
250 x 386   Scale 5½ft
WS III/XXI bottom L
Pen, pencil & pink wash
Holes for drainage and weights are marked A, B and
C. In Hawksmoor's hand.

144. *Section of NW tower and triforium*   S P 1 4 7
514 x 387   Scale 5½ft
WS III/XX L
Pen
Developed from No. 142.

145. *Elevation of W tower*   S P 1 5 5
613 x 240   Scale 5½ft
WS III/XIX R
Pen & grey wash
Developed from No. 142.

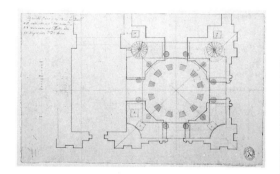

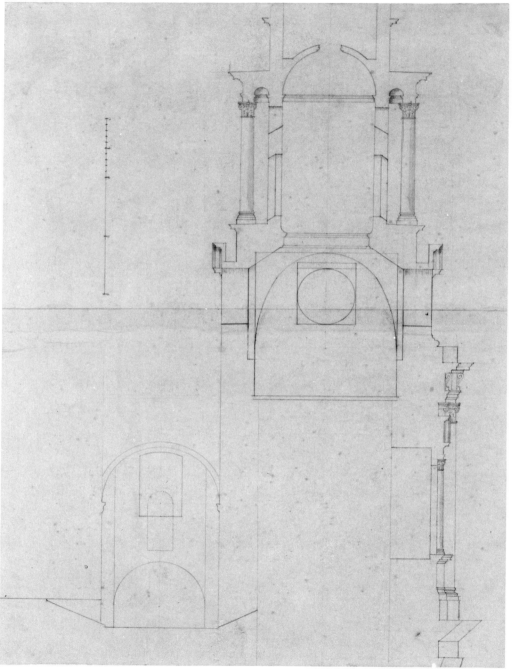

146. *Variant of No. 145*
383 x 250   Scale c. 5½ft
Pen & pencil

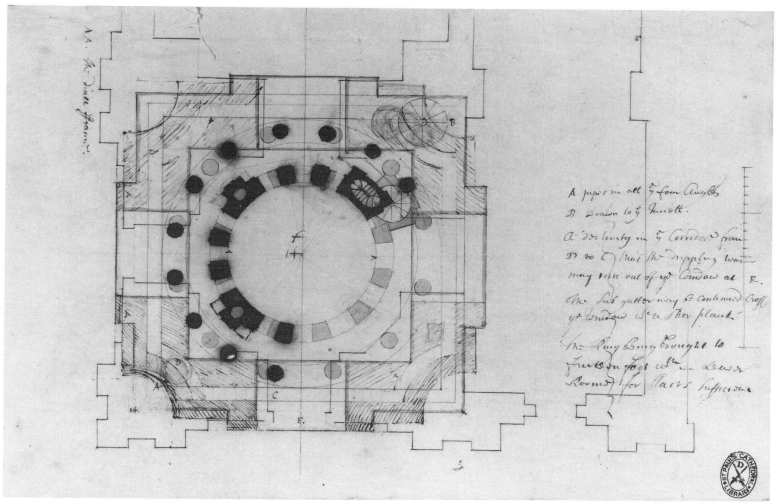

147. Similar design, elevation of clock stage   S P 1 5 6 B
242 x 310   Scale c.5½ft
Pen & pencil
L and R halves show alternative base levels for the peristyle, which in subsequent drawings begins higher up.

148. Revision of No. 143, NW tower   S P 1 5 1 B
248 x 382
WS III/XXI top L
Pen, pencil & brown wash
A link between the previous and following groups, showing the change from 12 to 16 columns in the peristyle. In Hawksmoor's hand.

147

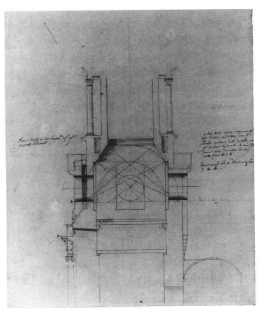

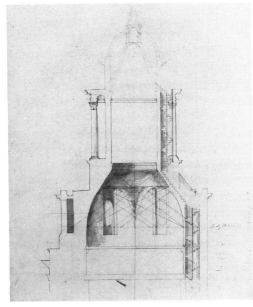

149. Revised section of NW tower and triforium SP 154
490 x 381   Scale 5½ft
WS III/XXII L
Pen & grey wash
Showing a taller clock stage than previous drawings. Annotated and perhaps drawn by William Dickinson, who joined the Cathedral office in 1696 and is first paid as a measurer.

150. Partial version of same design, SW tower SP 153
493 x 382   Scale 5½ft
WS III/XX R
Pencil, pen & grey wash

152. Section and half-elevation of W tower, 1702 design
SP 152
485 x 364   Scale c.5½ft
WS III/XVIII R
Pen, pencil & grey wash
The height has been further increased and corresponds with the authorized engraving of the W. front published in 1702. The peristyle has 16 columns. In spite of the confidence suggested by engraving, the heights were subsequently raised once again in the *verso* of No. 154 which became the core of the final design.

153. Revision of No. 148 SP 150
500 x 380   Scale c.5½ft
WS III/XXI R
Black-brown pen
Decidedly with 16 columns, and concordant with No. 152.

151. Diagonal section of W tower, similar design SP 157
492 x 382   Scale 5½ft
WS III/XXII R
Pen & grey wash
Same hand as No. 149. The lantern is shown with an internal cone, a miniature version of that adopted for the main dome.

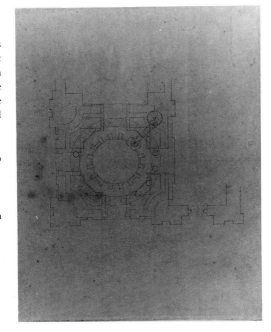

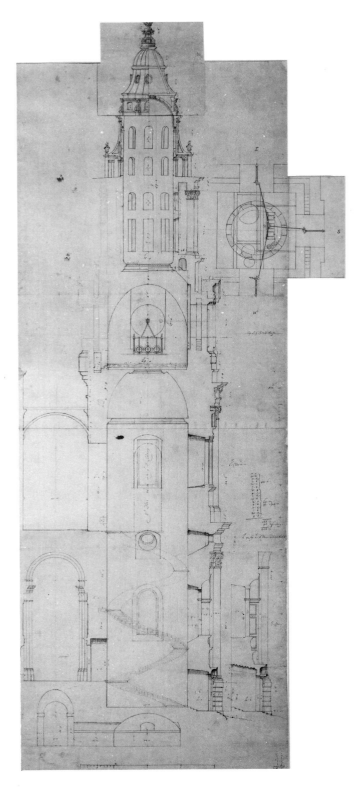

1137 x 445   Scale 5½ft

Pen & pencil

Made of several pieces pasted together. One of these, with an E-W section of the Library, is now mounted separately, measuring 235 x 340. There is also a plan of the clock stage. Annotated and perhaps partly drawn by Dickinson, but the drawing of the lead capping and finial is certainly Wren's. On the reverse of the sheet is a pen section, to the same scale, of the tower, with the lantern in pencil, similar to but higher than the 1702 engraved design (No. 152). Dickinson's note on the L side of this, *Concluded on Feb: 25th: 1703/4*, is placed in such a way as to suggest that it endorses the front rather than titling the back of the sheet. The design thus concluded upon involved a taller shell with more and different openings, grouped pillars in place of a regular peristyle, and a leaded wooden cap to the lantern of ogee profile. The *recto* drawing is consistent in all significant respects with the structure which began to rise above the church cornice in the spring of 1705. The drawing also shows the stone spiral stairway (the Geometrical Staircase) leading to the Library, which had just previously been set into the completed masonry cylinder of the tower.

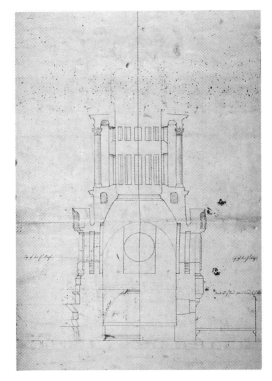

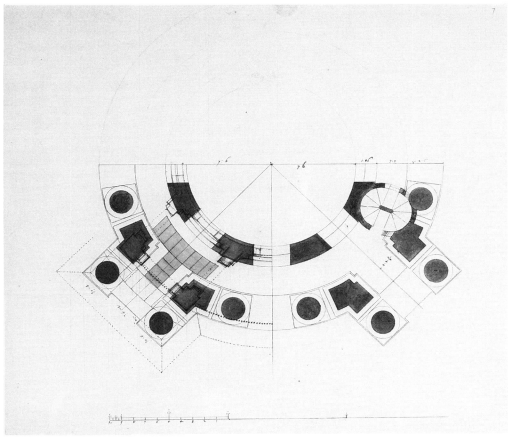

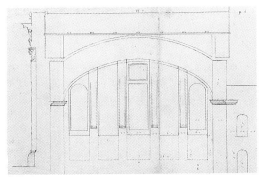

155. *Duplicate, clock and lantern stages of No. 154*

BUTE 9

486 x 376   Scale c.5½ft
Pen
Dated by Dickinson *Apr:22nd:1710* and endorsed by
him *Tower W. end St Paul's Church*. By 1710 the
towers were completed.

156. *Half-plan of one of the lanterns at colonnade stage*

BUTE 7

345 x 383
Pen & grey, red & yellow ink & grey wash
As executed.

By the summer of 1698 construction had reached the floor of the Whispering Gallery; at the end of 1700 it was up to the floor of the peristyle and it took another three years to reach the capitals of the small pilaster order of the piers. In the same period Wren had seen the making and printing of engravings which recorded a design that, above the peristyle, he would soon abandon. Nos. 157-162 relate to this critical period, but there must have been many other drawings for the dome that do not survive.

157. Studies for peristyle   SP111
643 x 790   Scale 4ft
WS III/V R
Pen, pencil & grey wash
Partly in Hawksmoor's hand. Section and part internal and external elevations of the peristyle level, not as executed. In particular the niches in the pier masses are placed too low; also a second tier of windows is shown inside the peristyle, as in Nos. 159-162. These were finally built as blind recesses. This sheet must have been superseded before the 1701 building season; subsequently (probably during 1702) Hawksmoor used the reverse for a

carefully ruled perspective of a canopied monument, reproduced (redrawn) in WS XIII/XXXII L as one of Wren's designs for an altar-canopy for St. Paul's. Apart from a fragmentary wooden model for a wall-attached altarpiece, all we know of Wren's altar designs is in the choir plan No. 166. The WS editors overlooked the significance of notes on two related plans at All Souls (IV.72, WS XIII/XXXI R, and IV.73). The latter is endorsed *Monument*; notes on the former identify *Linea Pedestall Equin*: Further drawings in the 1951 Bute sale, now in the V & A Museum, are in Hawksmoor's hand; one (E402-1951) shows an equestrian statue on the pedestal, and another (E399) is endorsed by Hawksmoor *Mausolea in honorem Guillemi iij.*

158. *Section of crossing and dome with alternatives*

SP 186/1

554 x 386   Scale c.12ft

WS XIII/XIII

Pencil & brown & red pen

L and R halves show alternative constructions; a flap gives a compromise between the two, but that on the L although closer to the fabric is only approximately correct. The R half differs markedly in the height of the inner dome, the lantern, and the stepped rings at the base of the outer dome. It also shows decorative frames and pilaster strips around the inside of the second tier of peristyle windows. In the flap this tier is retained but the inner dome is reduced in height. The L half shows a single course or moulding half-way up the zone of the upper windows, implying that they have been made blind.

If the earlier dome studies are any guide, it is probable that Wren proposed alternatives in this drawing, developed the R one as far as he could take it and then adopted the L one instead; this in itself is not an unreasonable or uncommon procedure. The lower part of the drawing may have been made earlier and discarded: it is unfinished, and the bay L of the dome contains a major error, being much too narrow. This is a more plausible interpretation than the suggestion in WS XIII, p. xv, that an otherwise unknown plan for the nave of 1685 is intentionally represented. The dimensions on the R, and probably some of the drawing, are in Dickinson's hand.

This and No. 164 were acquired from the collection of Sir Thomas Phillips by the RIBA for presentation to St Paul's in about 1935.

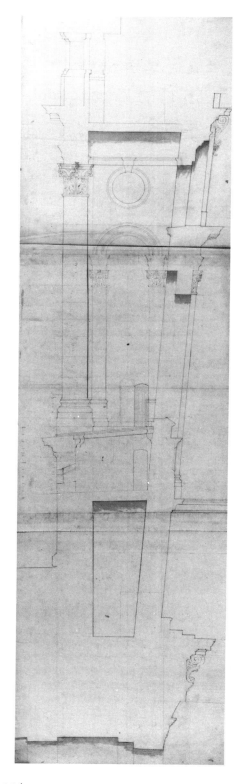

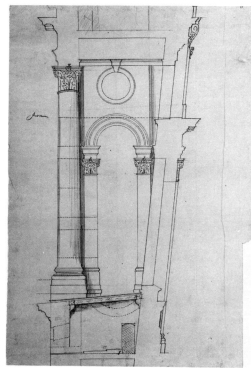

159. Section through drum and peristyle   SP 113
1405 x 388   Scale 2ft
WS III/V L
Pen, pencil & pink wash
Drawn by Hawksmoor. Agrees with the fabric up to the internal capitals, which were reached in the autumn of 1703.

160. Elevation, two bays inside peristyle   SP 169A
386 x 253   Scale 4ft
WS XIII/XIV L
Pen
Agrees with the fabric up to the internal capitals, except that the pilasters are fluted, not plain as executed. Fluting *in situ* was not uncommon, so a date between 1699 and 1703 is possible.

161. Section of peristyle   BUTE 6
387 x 249   Scale c.4ft
Pen
Similar to the upper part of No. 159, but shows more clearly the form of the exterior capitals with only one row of acanthus leaves. An iron chain is marked at the level of the internal cornice; it is mentioned in the 1705 accounts.

162. *Two bays of exterior peristyle*   BUTE 5

388 x 251   Scale c.4ft

Pen & grey wash

Revision of part of No. 157, showing the niches in the piers raised to the final level, but still with attic windows.

163. *Studies for an obelisk lantern*   SP 51

474 x 341   Scale 5ft

WS II/XIX

Pen

On the L a taller obelisk of the same base size (8ft) and 60ft high. Probably by Hawksmoor who had a liking for obelisks. The diameter of 25ft is compatible with the lantern over the dome, and the division into eight segments is compatible with this. No comparable studies are known, and the alternative suggestion in WS that this drawing may be related to the W towers cannot be sustained.

164. *Half-section, top of cone and lantern*   SP 186/2

490 x 365   Scale 4ft

WS XIII/XIV R

Pen, pencil & grey wash

The L half of the sheet contains the setting-out of a plan at the level of the uppermost cone windows. The cone was completed in 1707 and this drawing, which shows only the masonry, and does not conform to the fabric in details, can be no later.

For provenance see No. 158.

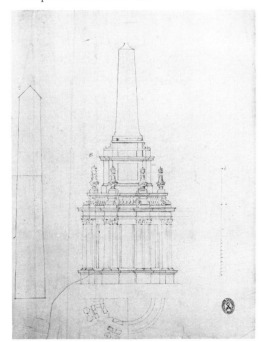

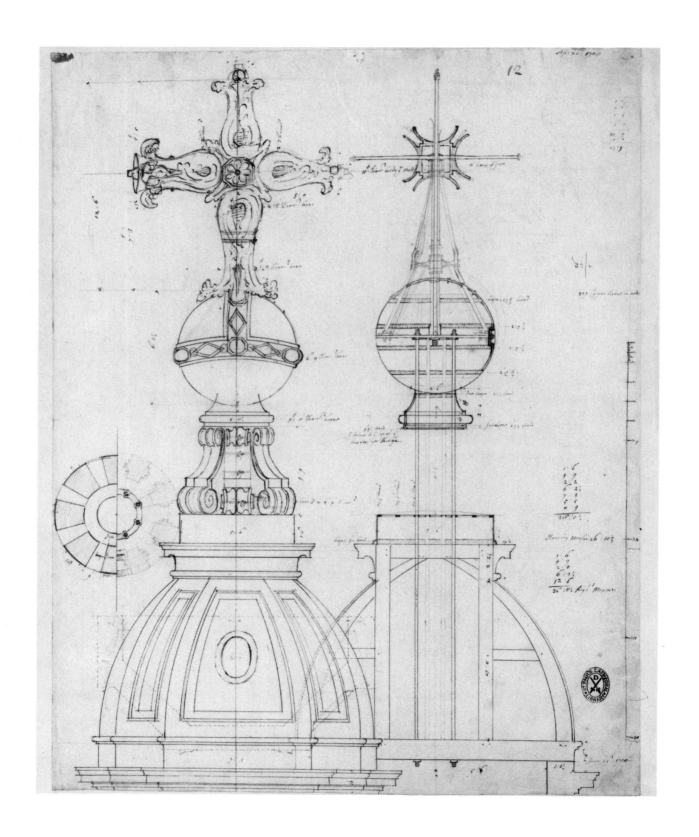

165. Details of lantern: cap, ball and cross   SP 44

487 x 371   Scale 2ft

WS II/XIV

Pencil & pen

Annotated by Dickinson. Dated at top *Ap:26 1708* and at bottom *June 29th 1708*. On the reverse is an estimate by Dickinson dated 10 November for the gilding of the cap.

The Building Commission, at its meeting of 1 May 1694, saw Wren's designs for the furnishing of the choir and ordered them to be put in hand as soon as conveniently possible. Their committee held a further meeting on 10 May and discussed, among other matters, the provision of the organ, whose screen, placed across the axis of the W bay of the choir, formed an important part of the furnishings, from the first service in the choir on 2 December 1697 until its removal in 1861. In 1872 the organ case, split into two, was rebuilt in the present positions on either side of the E arch of the dome. The choir stalls were moved a whole bay further W and the floor was raised by 2½ft. Before these changes the wooden structures were surveyed by F. C. Penrose, whose drawings are reproduced in WS XVI/X-XV. Besides the drawings in this section (Nos. 166-179) there are a number for the organ case (Nos. 180-186) and other details (Nos. 187-189). Some of the drawings are in part or in whole by craftsmen rather than the Surveyor's staff.

166. S half-plan of choir showing stalls and altar

BUTE 19

1110 x 525   Scale 5½ft

Pencil

Corresponds in general to Penrose's survey (WS XVI/X) but with several specific differences: (1) The Bishop's throne in the E stall and the canopied throne in the middle stall are not as executed. (2) The steps at the E end of the stalls and at the altar rail are curved instead of straight. (3) An altarpiece flanked by piers and columns is shown, standing 10ft in front of the E window; this was not constructed, for it is not shown in Trevitt's engraved view of the choir as in 1706. (4) At the W end there is a suggestion, in faint quadrant lines, of the alternative semi-circular return stalls that are elaborated in elevation drawings Nos. 174, 178 and 179. This drawing must precede the design produced by Wren on 1 May 1694.

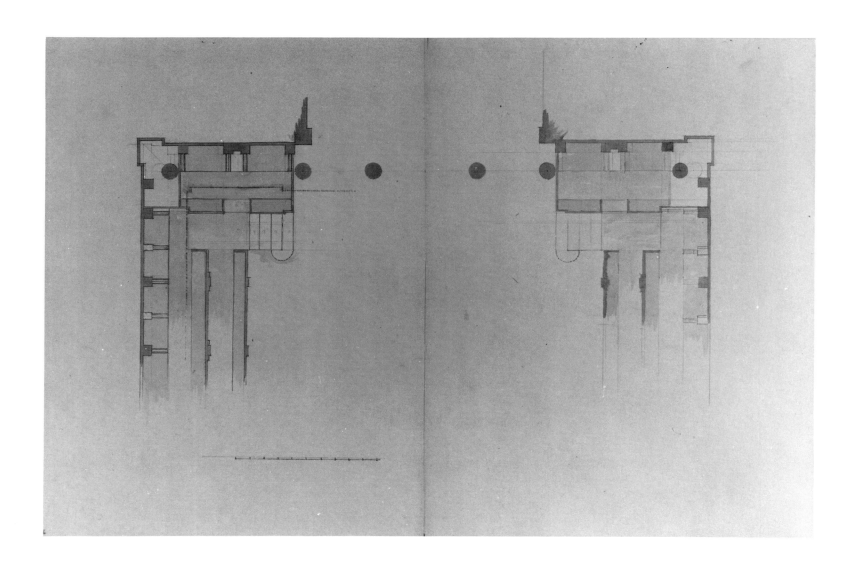

167. Plan of W. end return stalls BUTE 20
468 x 707   Scale 2ft
Pen, pencil, grey & yellow wash
Only roughly as executed.

168. Plan of one bay of stalls SP 78
366 x 515   Scale 2ft
Pen & pencil
Inscribed: *Choire Plan of one Bay.* As executed except
that the stall entrances are differently placed.

169. Duplicate of No. 168 BUTE 21
381 x 527   Scale 2ft
Pen

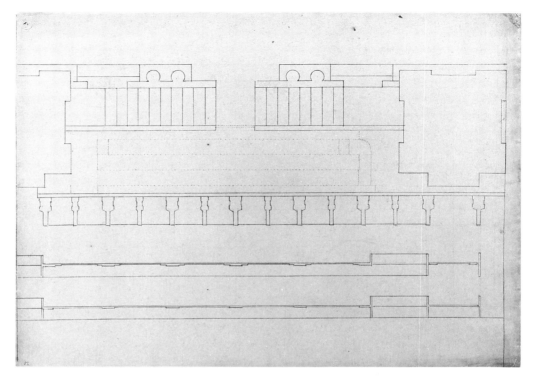

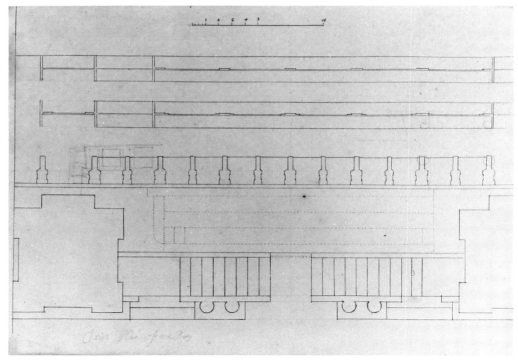

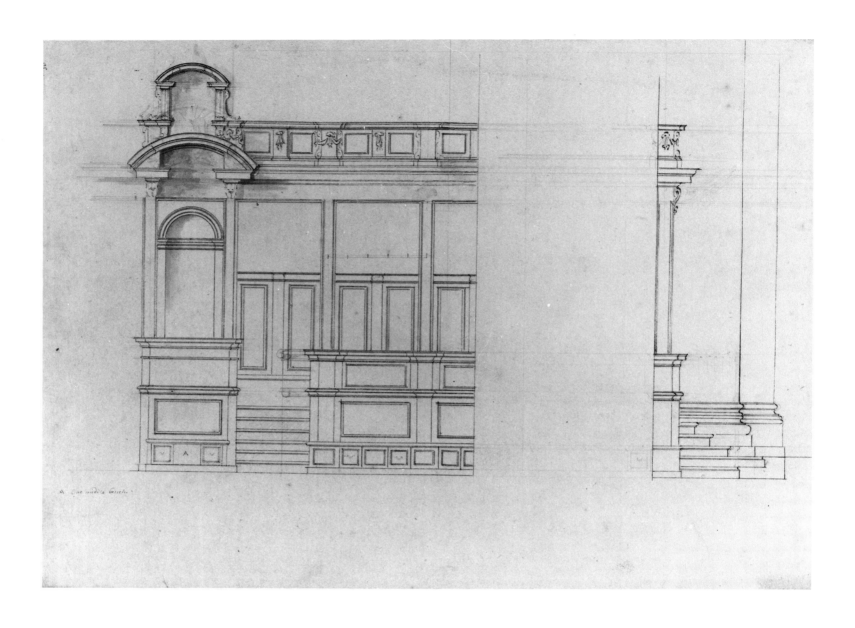

170. Part elevation and end of stalls   SP 82

371 x 506   Scale 2ft

WS II/XXVII

Pen, pencil & grey wash

Stall levels, panelling and enrichment are not finalised. A note *A One middle bench* refers to the base of the canopied seat and to the extra seats which retracted on lignum vitae rollers. These were admired by Evelyn (*Diary*, 5 October 1694) but either he saw a model on that occasion or, as was often the case, he revised his diary entry some time after his visit. His editor, E. S. de Beer, suggested that the sliding seats were experimental and perhaps not executed; however, the December 1695 account includes £18 to Edward Sherlock "For 36 Lignum Vitae Wheels & Steel-spindles for ye Drawing Seats in the Choir".

171. Detail of canopy in No. 170   SP 85

510 x 375   Scale c.1:6

WS II/XXIX upper

Pencil, pen & grey wash

Inscribed: *The Bp's Throne and my Ld Mayors* and *Resolved upon*. For the Lord Mayor's seat in the middle stall and the one facing it; the Bishop's throne at the E has a different canopy. Alternatives were carefully drawn in pencil; that on the R was crossed out and that on the L developed in pen. Similar ideas to the R half can be found in No. 183 *verso*.

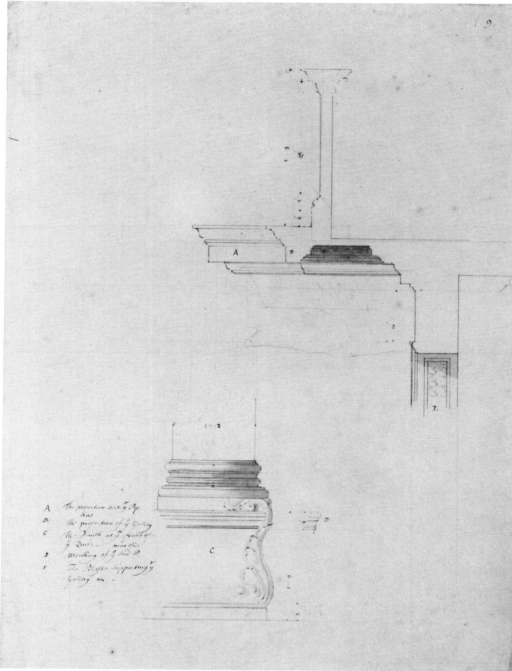

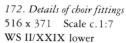

172. *Details of choir fittings*   SP 86

516 x 371   Scale c.1:7

WS II/XXIX lower

Pencil, pen & grey wash

Above, detail section of gallery adjoining a canopy. Below, detail of column base and pedestal of choir screen; moulding of pedestal. Probably by Hawksmoor including the annotated key. The columns and their marble pedestals were incorporated, after the demolition of the screen, into the N and S transept inside porches; those in the S survived the Second World War and are *in situ*.

Fig. 169

173. *Full-size plan of a stall pilaster*   BUTE 26

527 x 375

Pen

Inscribed: *Pillar between ye Stauls*. At the bottom of the drawing is either an arm rest or a canopy support, depending on the level represented.

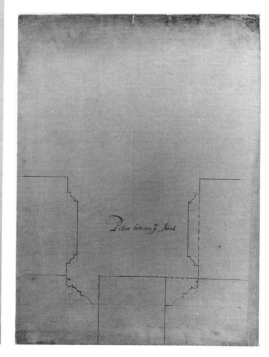

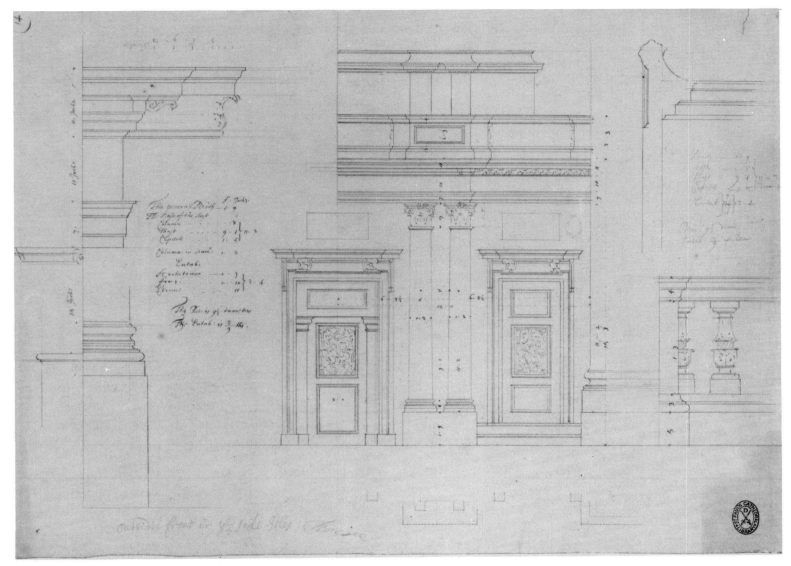

174. Half-elevation and details of one choir aisle screen

SP 81

370 x 510   Scale 2ft and 1:6
WS II/XXVI
Pen
Inscribed in pencil: *outsidie front in ye side. Isles Choire*.
From L to R (above): entablature; half-elevation;
parapet; (below): base; plan of carpentry; balustrade.
Corresponds to the fabric in general but not in detail
disposition.

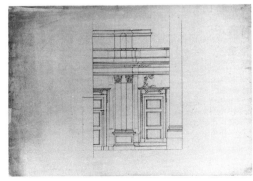

175. Half-elevation of choir aisle screen   BUTE 22

381 x 527   Scale 2ft
Pen & pencil
Alternative to the main drawing in No. 174.

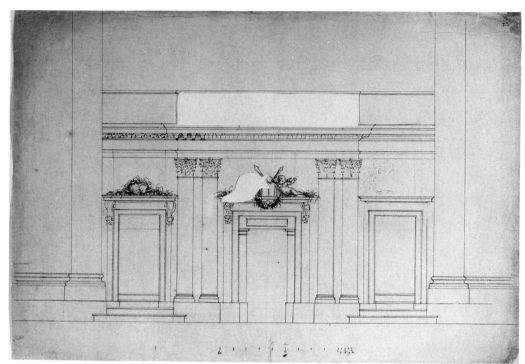

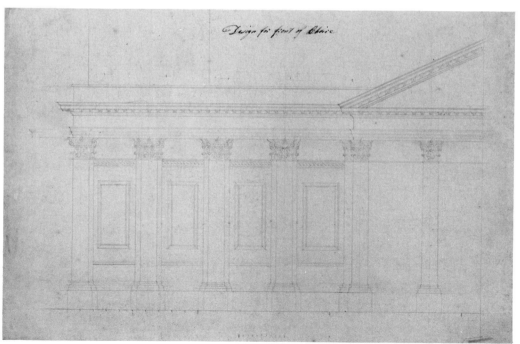

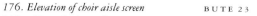

176. Elevation of choir aisle screen   BUTE 23
380 x 527   Scale c. 2ft
Pen, pencil & brown wash
Alternative to Nos. 174-175, not as executed. Some of the detail probably by Grinling Gibbons. Two portions of the carving have been cut out.

177. Half W elevation of choir screen   SP 79
345 x 514   Scale c. 6ft
WS II/XXIV
Pencil
Inscribed in a later hand: *Design for front of Choire*. Above the parapet, plan of the order to a smaller scale. The panelling differed in execution and the pilasters were not fasciated.

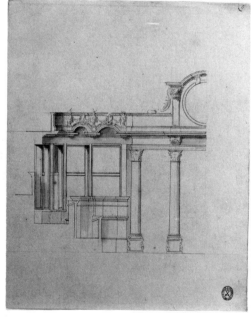

179. Half E elevation of screen and return stalls   SP 83
494 x 379   Scale 2ft
WS II/XXVIII upper
Pen & grey wash
Corresponds to No. 178. For the chair organ case in the middle see Nos. 180-181.

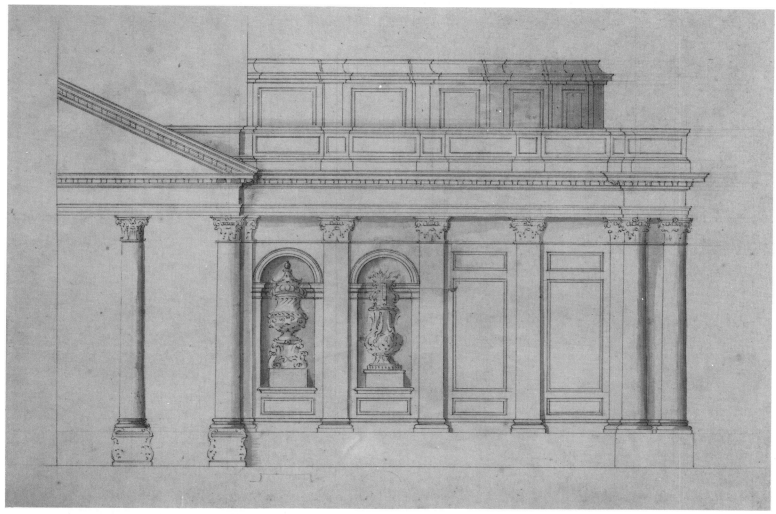

178. Half W elevation of choir screen   SP 80
348 x 494   Scale 2ft
WS II/XXV
Pen & grey wash
Shows the marble floral bases to the columns as built.
The quadrant returns visible in No. 166 appear above
the screen.

Bernard Smith's contract for the organ was approved and confirmed on 19 December 1694; he was to complete the organ by 25 March 1696 "in ye Case that shall be set up and provided with all Ornaments, Carvings and Gilding". In the 19th century a mythology arose to the effect that Wren disliked organs in general and Smith in particular, that the case was made too small, *etcetera*. In fact the Committee decided on 10 May 1694 after consultations with Smith and Dr Blow the organist that the organ should be 22ft high by 18ft wide by 6ft deep: these dimensions can be accommodated, allowing the thickness of the casework, within both the completed structure and that shown in No. 180. It is not uncommon for either organs or other kinds of mechanism to be difficult to fit in practice into the containers intended for them and in fact Smith's own estimate was over-optimistic. It is usually, and probably wrongly, assumed that Wren heightened the case after a decision to extend the compass from FFF down to CCC. In recent years it has been suggested that the screen could or should be rebuilt and the organ placed on it once more. While this would do wonders for the understanding of Wren's conception and would have the incidental advantage of screening from view the neo-Baroque altar canopy, it is not practically possible to make such a reconstruction any more than it is feasible to recreate within St Paul's the conditions of 18th-century life or liturgy. Nevertheless historians should represent the original intentions and appearances as far as they are known. An anonymous broadside of c.1700 suggested that Wren would have liked "a free and airy Prospect of the whole length of the church" (BL 816 m.9(93), reprinted *Camden Soc.*, n.s.XXVI (1880), p.165); this suggestion also was made by the Dean, H. H. Milman (*Annals of S. Paul's Cathedral*, 1869, p.435) on the basis of our No. 186, which shows a small organ case under one of the choir arches. Penrose, who found this drawing, misunderstood the dimensional problems involved and drew support for his idea from the fact that the piers in the crypt under the screen were a last-minute addition. This is quite true — the centre arch was turned in June 1695 — but in view of the open ended conduct of the whole St Paul's project and the constant uncertainty about money it would have been imprudent of Wren to have built in supports for an organ in advance of the decision to have one. Penrose may well have believed that, as with the W. steps (see No. 136), he was reviving Wren's intentions in removing the screen. That (to use Mies van der Rohe's antithesis) would have been a *good* reason, but the *real*

reason was that the clergy now wanted a vista from the nave through the choir, both musical and architectural, to the altar.

Drawings for the organ show a series of sliding sash-frames in front of the pipes; the accounts show that these were installed with pulleys and weights, and engravings record their appearance. It was common for Italian and Dutch organ cases to have closing shutters on hinges, as much for liturgical and decorative reasons, like the wings of triptychs, as for practical ones. Initially the problem at St Paul's was dust: work continued on the building even for some years after it was deemed complete in 1710, and dust is the enemy of mechanisms and speaking pipes alike. Eventually the sashes became troublesome and were taken out; fragments survive.

180. Section through choir with E elevation of organ

495 x 360   Scale 4ft
Pen, pencil & grey wash
Not as executed, but similar in dimensions and general outline, and showing straight return stalls and marble column bases.

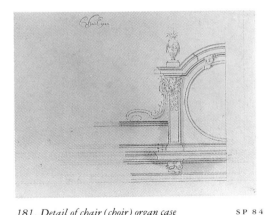

181. Detail of chair (choir) organ case
368 x 464   Scale c.1:10
Pencil, pen & grey wash
Placed behind (E of) the organist's seat: hence *chair organ*, generally corrupted to *choir* but known in German as *Rückpositiv*. The same design as in Nos. 179-180.

182. Study for organ case
476 x 345   Scale c.1ft
WS II/XXXI
Pencil & pen
The largest pipes are only 8ft pitch, the fundamental

bass of a substantial organ of the time being 16ft. Possibly a design for a small organ, but more probably for the lower side face of the main case: No. 180 shows pedimented projections of the right size.

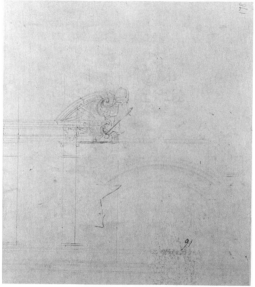

183. Study for one of the case towers   S P 1 7 8
351 x 294   Scale 1ft
WS III/XXXIV L
Pencil, pen & grey wash
The crown is more appropriate to the organ case (see
Nos. 185-186) than to the Bishop's or Lord Mayor's
thrones; in addition if the scale is correct the width
would fit No. 180.

The pencil sketch on the reverse is less identifiable,
showing part of a pedimented entablature carried on
pillars. It does not relate closely to any other drawings
for the organ, or to No. 171, but in proportions it is
not unlike No. 184.

184. Elevation of part of an organ case   S P 1 7 9
624 x 511   Scale 1ft
WS III/XXXIV upper
Pen & grey wash

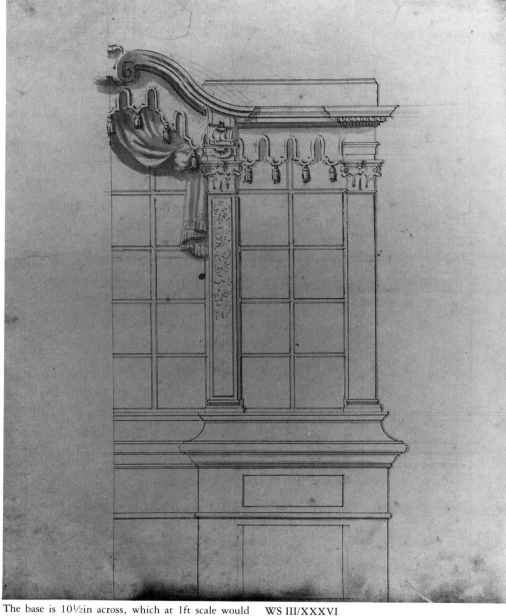

The base is 10½in across, which at 1ft scale would
give a width of 21ft, which is compatible with a
slightly wider case than the one shown in No. 180
and with a different internal disposition. The motif of
carved curtains drawn back is common to both
drawings.

185. Alternative to No. 184   S P 1 8 3
527 x 381   Scale 2ft?

WS III/XXXVI
Pencil, pen & grey wash
The detail is in the hand of Grinling Gibbons, who
carved the executed case. Medallions show a king and
queen, appropriate before the death of Queen Mary in
December 1694; the finials are alternatives. The same
drawn curtains appear as in the preceding drawing
and No. 180, and at 2ft scale the case is only
fractionally wider than in No. 180 and the right
shape for the upper part.

168

170

186. *Elevation of a small organ case under an arch*   SP 184
381 x 525   Scale c. 2ft
WS III/XXXVII
Pen & brown ink wash
The base line is the parapet over the stalls. The detail drawn by Grinling Gibbons. The two sides are alternatives and the R has a queen's head as in No. 185. It is clear that an organ under one of the choir arches was considered; the more ambitious idea of paired instruments on both sides of the choir is not likely, since it would have required two players before the advent of pneumatic action. The problem of size, however, was a serious one, since pipes of more than 12ft pitch would not fit comfortably or credibly into a case of this height. The outline of the arch establishes the scale beyond doubt. Would-be buyers of organs often pass through a period of parsimony and ignorance to one of extravagant enthusiasm which has, in turn, to be tempered by greater realism. This drawing perhaps represents, through the carver's hand, the architect's response to the first of these three phases.

187—189. OTHER DETAIL SKETCHES
FOR THE CHOIR

187. *Sketch for a canopy*   SP 182B
240 x 326
WS III/XXXV bottom R
Pen & pencil
Probably a carver's design for the Bishop's throne. There are further pen and pencil sketches on the reverse.

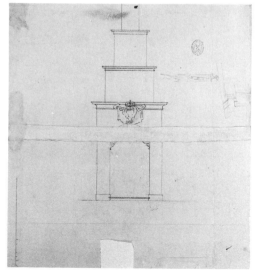

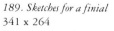

188. Sketch for a canopy   BUTE 25

440 x 354

Pencil, pen & grey wash

The topmost decoration has been cut out. On the reverse is a curious elevation of a structure of four stages, partly overlaid by an old repair strip. According to a scale at bottom L the first stage is 23ft high with an arch 9ft wide; this is surmounted by a cartouche set on a drape with a crown over it. The impression is given of a wooden rather than a masonry structure.

189. Sketches for a finial   BUTE 24

341 x 264

Pen & grey wash

Four finials of similar appearance are shown above the return stalls in No. 180. An alternative is drawn on a flap, now separately mounted on the sheet.

The NW chapel (now St Dustan's) was originally designated the Morning Prayer Chapel; the SW (now of St Michael and St George) was originally furnished for the Consistory Court. It is of course a myth that these spaces were added to the design in 1685 at the behest of James II to make the Cathedral suitable for Roman Catholic worship. This idea is based on ignorance both of the building history and of the Roman liturgy, for which the "cathedral form", demanded by the Chapter because of its reminiscence of the medieval building, would have been eminently suitable. The furnishing of the Morning Prayer Chapel was concurrent with that of the choir.

190. Plan for seating and steps　　　SP 18

371 x 526　Scale c. 3ft

WS XIII/XX

Pencil, pen & grey & yellow wash

Probably drawn by Dickinson, who inscribed it *Morning prayr Chappell* and in pencil *Pave with sweeds arras way* (i.e. Swedish paving stones set diagonally). There is also a key to the letters on the drawing, of which *E* indicates the reading pew under the N window. The chapel has since been refurnished, but originally No. 190 was probably followed exactly, since it agrees with the plan shown in No. 202.

191. Project for wrought-iron screen　　　BUTE 27

252 x 378　Scale 2ft

Pencil & pen

Half-elevation. Inscribed R: *A Lower*, referring to the horizontal bar at the top of the column bases. On the L a sketch of wall panelling and seats. A wooden screen was provided: see No. 192.

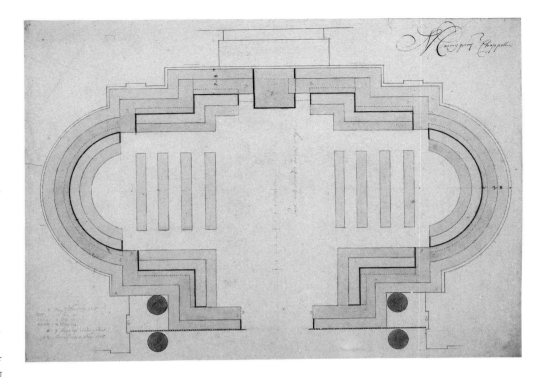

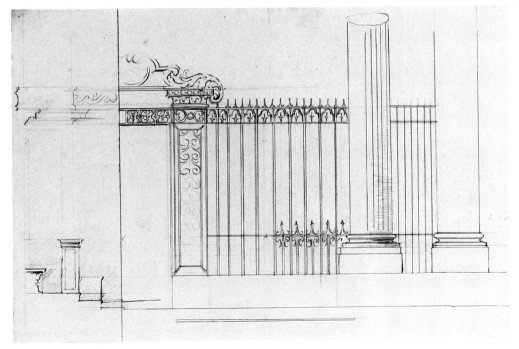

192. *Design for wooden screen*   BUTE 28
521 x 345   Scale c.1:22
Pen, pencil & grey wash
Endorsed: *Entrance to the chaple S.P.* Mostly as executed, including the low iron railing shown in the L half.

193. *Sketch for spandrel under a quarter-gallery*   SP 177 B
330 x 412
WS III/XXXIII lower
Pen & pencil
Probably by Grinling Gibbons, who was paid for carving these spandrels in July 1694.

194. *Design for altar-rail and gate*   SP 89
355 x 412   Scale c.1:6
WS II/XXXII upper
Pen, pencil & grey wash
Inscribed, probably by Hawksmoor: *Summum Altare Paulinu–*. Not as executed: Trevitt's engraving of the choir as in 1706 shows a metal railing across the apse.

195. *Sketch for a lamp*   SP 90
352 x 230
WS II/XXXII lower
Pen & pencil
Inscribed: *Chandelier pour la Eglise de St. Paul. London Octob: 21. 1967.* The form *la Eglise* suggests a communication to rather than from a French speaker. In March 1698 Mary Sherlock, widow of Edward, was paid £40 for "2 Brass Branches & 2 Lanthorns". Trevitt's view shows two hanging candelabra.

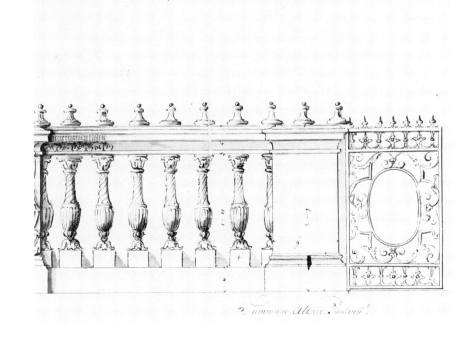

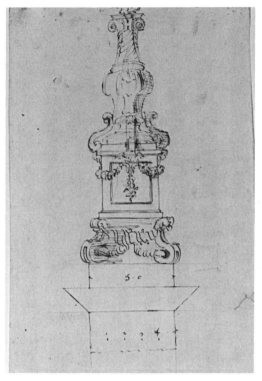

196. Sketches for finials   S P 1 8 0
300 x 192 and 301 x 190
WS III/XXXV L
Pen & pencil
These are large objects on bases 5ft wide, presumably
for the outside of the building and suggesting both
the hand and the imagination of Hawksmoor. See also
No. 197.

197. Sketches for finials   S P 1 8 1
298 x 192 and 300 x 192
WS III/XXXV centre (in reverse order)
Pen & pencil
Alternatives to No. 196.

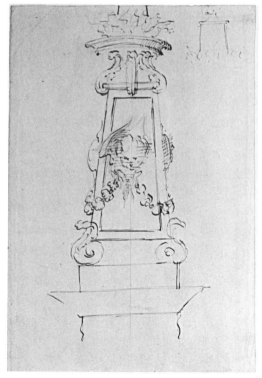

198. Sketch for decoration over Dean's Door   SP 182A
209 x 330   Scale c.1ft
WS III/XXXV upper
Pen & grey wash
Not as executed but showing a simpler version of motifs used.

199. Sketches for spandrel reliefs   SP 185
343 x 503
WS III/XII R
Pencil, grey pen & wash
Two drawings on one sheet. Above, half one of the soffits over the clerestory windows. Below, half one of the keystones of the main arches under the dome. Neither as executed. The soffits were executed in plaster but the keystones were carved by Cibber in 1698. Both the medium and the draughtsmanship are unusual, but although the drawings have a rococo delicacy it is hard to believe that they would have been made after the keystones had been finished.

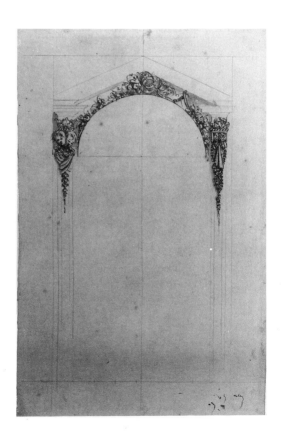

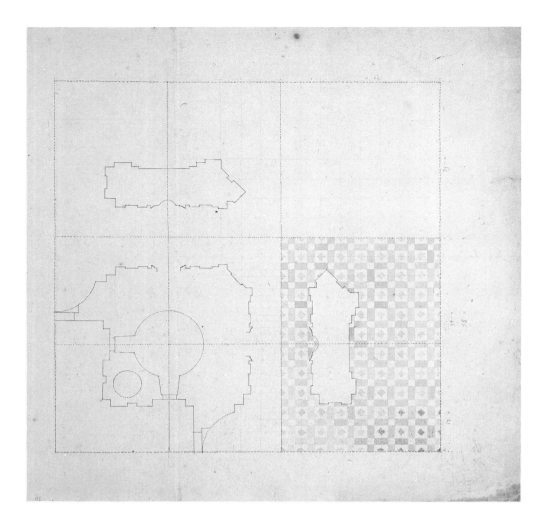

200. Quarter-plan of crossing with proposal for paving

BUTE 30

530 x 530   Scale c.6ft

Pen & grey & yellow wash

The circular core of the bastion implies the SW quarter, but blank drawings were not always used so precisely (see No. 108). The proposal, for a pattern of lozenges within squares, was not carried out. Annotated bottom L: *The genll sqs are 4.10½ Small Sqrs are 1.7½ The line A falls 18' to the Right hand.*

201. SE quarter-plan of crossing with alternatives   SP17

492 x 722   Scale c.4ft

WS II/VII

Pen & brown & grey wash

Annotated and dimensioned: four alternative sixteenths shown under the dome, of which the second clockwise was executed. Inscribed below the diagonal arch: *Dec 9th 1708 — White.* Endorsed, in respect of the executed portion (marked A): *Memndum. the 16th part A, as expressed by ye plan is approved by Sr Chr Wren Knt, the 27th March 1707.*

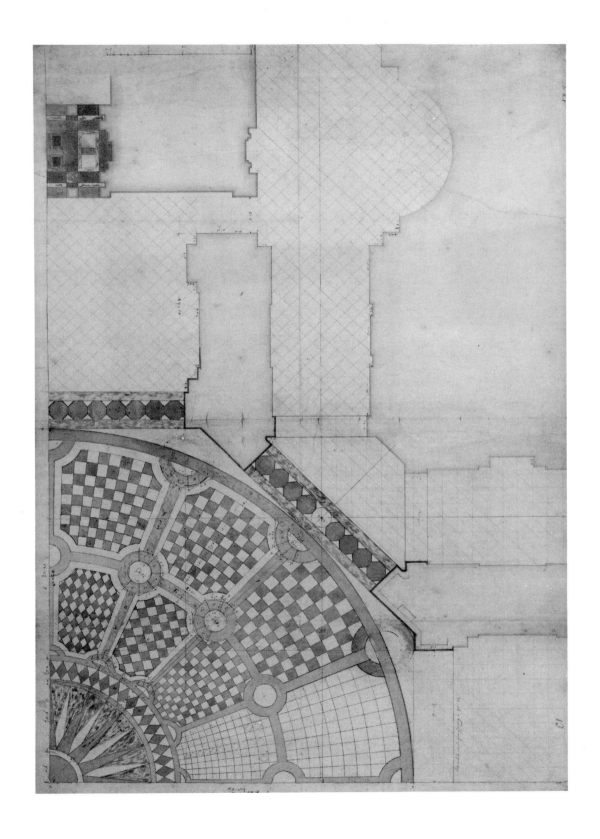

202. *Complete paving plan, as executed*   BUTE 29
1625 x 804   Scale 10ft
Pen & grey, yellow & red wash
Probably by Dickinson. Certainly made after No. 201
(which shows alternatives) and therefore probably
after completion, though the making of such a
drawing, whether or not as a record, is without
precedent.

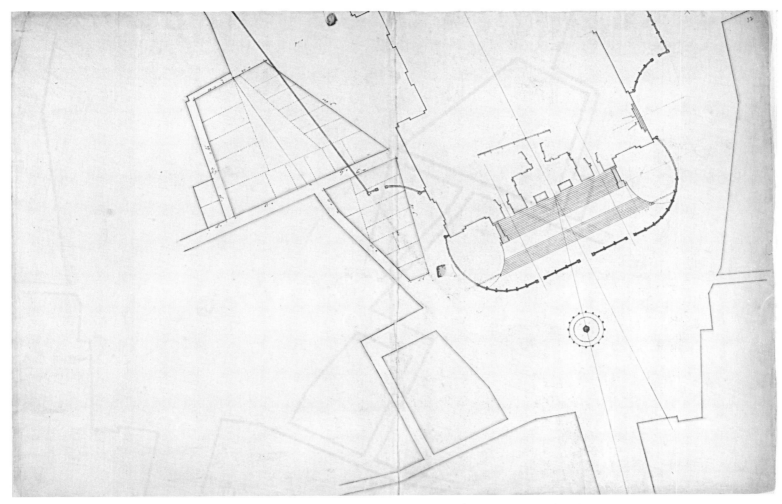

203. Plan of W end and environs   BUTE 32
506 x 760   Scale c.20ft
Pen & yellow & red wash
By William Dickinson. Showing the proposed line of the churchyard railing, with Queen Anne's monument placed on the line of Ludgate Hill. Dated on the reverse 24 February 1709/10, with a reference to the cast-iron fence for which Richard Jones contracted.

204. Plan of proposed enclosure of N portico   SP 10
310 x 505   Scale c.8ft
WS II/VI lower (wrongly described)
Pen & grey wash
By Dickinson. Dated 2 April 1713. Wren was no longer attending the Commission.

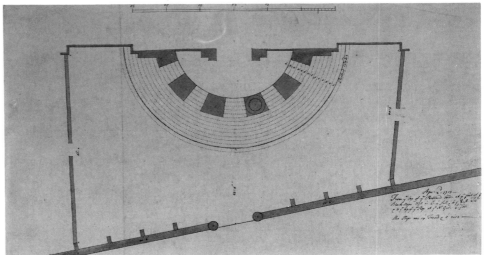

182

205. *W elevation, preparatory to Gribelin's 1702 print*

SP 49

890 x 850   Scale 10ft
WS II/XVII
Black pen & pencil

A damaged endorsement at the top reads: *recommenda
[ombre] a gauche pour que les impressions . . . a droite.*
There are pencil notes *coll* and *pill* to show columns to
be shaded to indicate roundness in contrast to flat
pilasters. The endorsement refers to the reversal of
cast shadows in printing, and the language may be
accounted for by Gribelin's Huguenot origin. The
drawing, of which the upper half is probably later
than the lower, lacks many decorative details found in
the print, and also shows niches instead of windows in
the second storey of the towers. In that respect a
drawing at All Souls (II.39, Fig. XVIII) is closer to
the engraving; however, the All Souls drawing, which
is made up with scissors and paste, differs in the clock
stages.

206. *Plans of dome and W tower*

SP 16

720 x 520   Scale 11ft
Grey pen & wash

Plans of (a) drum above peristyle; (b) W tower at
peristyle; (c) dome peristyle. As executed. The
selection of subjects suggests a record, but no
engraving is known that embodies them.

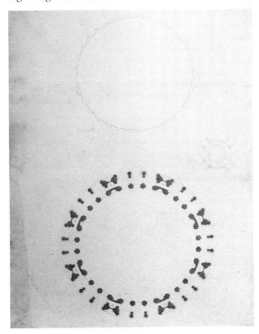

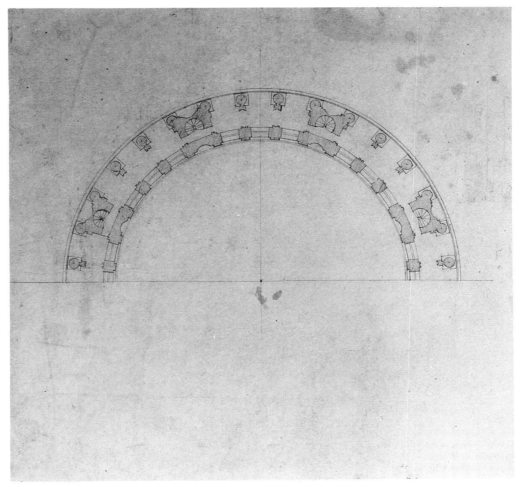

207. *Half-plan of peristyle*

SP 112B

239 x 248   Scale 20ft
Pen

As executed. Purpose unknown, but see note to No.
206. The scale is that used for most of the early dome
studies, but this drawing records the final design.

208. *Preparation for perspective from NW*

BUTE 18

492 x 388
Pencil

Part of W front and transept end and some
construction lines. From the same angular viewpoint,
though not the same level, as Robert Trevitt's
*Scenographia Templi Paulini a Parte Occidentali ad
Borealem*, which probably dates from 1710. He was
paid in July 1710 (transcribed in WS XV, p.192 as
Trent) for drawing and engraving the choir in 1706
and "in Perspective the Outside View of the Church".
see over

183

209. "Mr Flitcroft's Plan of the Peers" 1752   S P 1 9
438 x 362   Scale c. 11½ft
WS II/VIII
Black pen & grey wash
Plan of the SE quarter of the crossing. The E pier of
the S transept arch is marked A, and the drawing is
inscribed *A the peer which has been Repaired*. It is
endorsed *Mr Flitcrofts plan of the Peers on the South side of
the Church between the middle & side Isles Aug 1752*.
Flitcroft was Surveyor 1746-56 and was responsible
for the repair of a pier in which the rubble core had
settled.

210. Plan of SE quarter of the building   S P 9 4
350 x 522   Scale c. 11½ft
WS III/II upper
Pen & black wash
Inscribed: *note the walls are 14 foot thick*. Exactly
dimensioned survey drawing. Technically similar,
though inferior, to No. 209 and to the same scale.

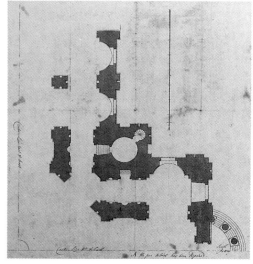

184

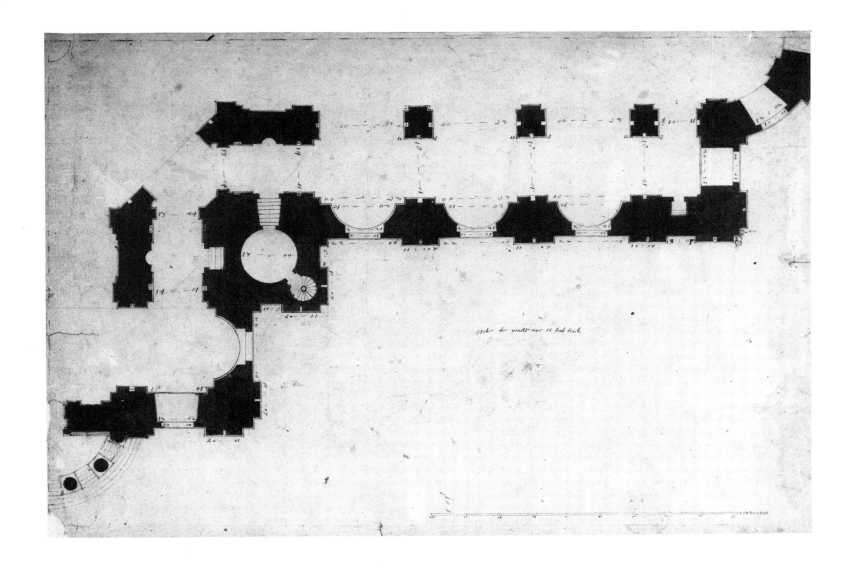

DIV. PAVL. DOM.

*Entry made by an Ascent of
Flagg Tdoewayes.*

*The pillars are 3 out of ye wall
and that the Cupola of S. Architrave
may not too much a strong both
be set 6 inches within ye upright
of ye pillar*

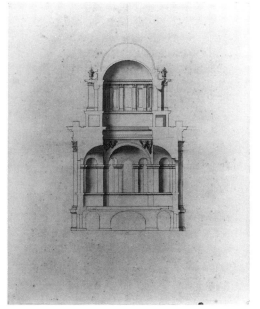

By 1710 Hawksmoor had begun to establish an
independent practice; he was also increasingly
interested in environments and complexes of
buildings, and in the next few years would produce
hopeful proposals for the replanning of Oxford and
Cambridge and the addition of a great chapel and
courtyard to Greenwich Hospital. This seems also to be
the date of schemes in his hand for a domed building
at the top of Ludgate Hill and a four-storey sequence
of buildings around the churchyard, forming a bell-
shaped enclosure. The drawings are all autograph and
have his comments, and there is no reason to connect
any of them with Wren, who must have taken a
detached view of a project which, for all its grandeur,
was quite unrealistic in the climate of the time.
Indeed he may already have stopped attending
Commission meetings before Hawksmoor drew out
his scheme. The domed building is more probably a
baptistery than a chapter house – Hawksmoor was
well aware of the long tradition of round domed
buildings for this purpose. Both in architectural style
and in draughtsmanship the designs for it are close to
some of his drawings of c.1711-12 for the circular
Radcliffe Library in Oxford.

211. Half-section, plan and elevation of baptistery S P 1 5 8
483 x 374   Scale c.9ft
WS III/XXIII
Pen & grey wash

212. Elevation of the same   S P 1 5 9
480 x 373   Scale 9½ft
WS III/XXIV L
Pen & grey wash

213. Section of the same   S P 1 6 0
481 x 374   Scale 9½ft
WS III/XXIV R
Pen & grey wash

214. Plan for churchyard   S P 1 7 3
623 x 1112   Scale c.25ft
WS III/XXXI lower
Pen & grey wash
At the top of Ludgate Hill is the plan of a building
very like that shown in plan No. 211.

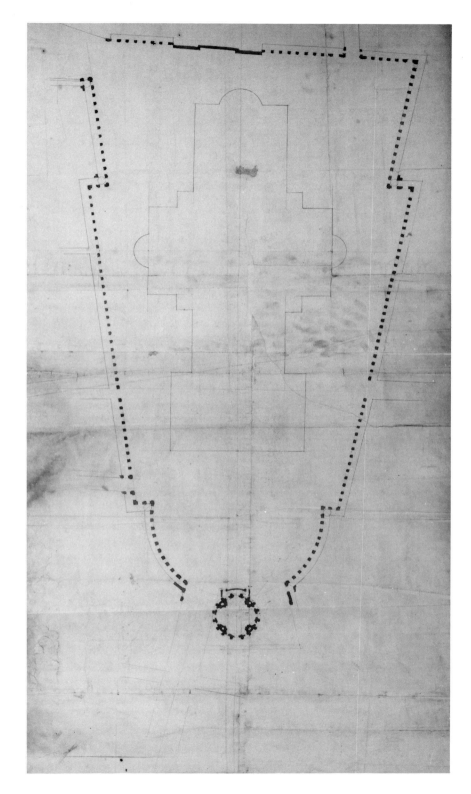

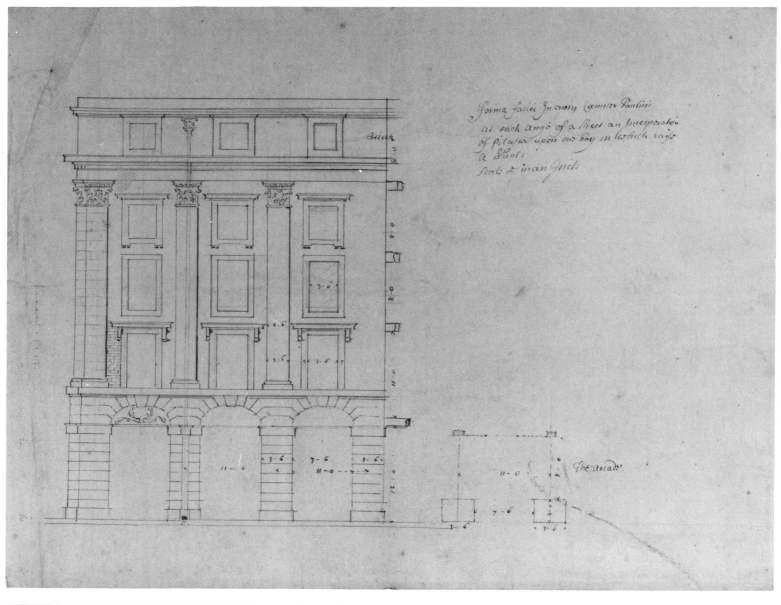

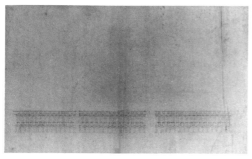

215. *Elevation of S side of churchyard*
493 × 750   Scale 20ft
WS III/XXXII upper
Pencil

216. *Three end bays of one block*
375 × 485   Scale 5ft
WS III/XXXII lower
Pen & pencil
Inscribed: *forma faciei Interioris coemeter Paulini*. The arches have blind tympana as in Wren's Trinity College Library.

217. Elevation of one bay at one of the angles   S P 1 7 6
500 x 385   Scale 5ft
WS XIII/XXXIII
Pencil
Inscribed in pen: *AA The Turrets and duplicacoin of pilasters at ye Angles, Vide plan.*

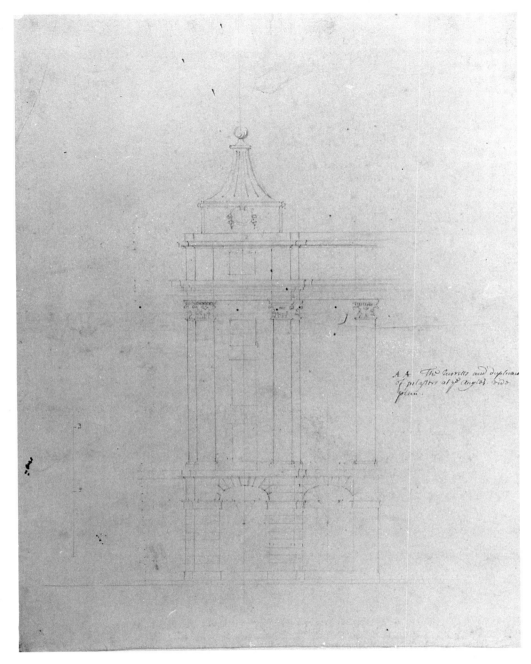

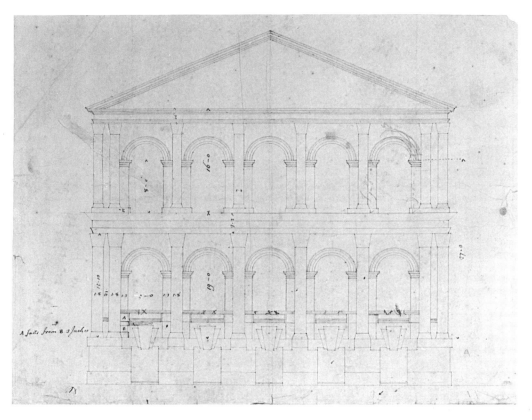

218. Half-plan at several levels, steeple of St Bride, Fleet Street   BUTE 4

83 x 233   Scale c.4½ft

Pen & pencil

More or less as executed. St Bride's steeple was added in 1702-03. The identification is due to Robert Crayford.

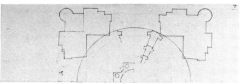

219. Hawksmoor: N front of St George, Bloomsbury   SP 142

379 x 470   Scale 4ft

WS III/XVI

Pen

Misidentified in WS as the Sheldonian Theatre; though corrected in Vol. XX and elsewhere, the error has led to the persistence of an idea that Wren's original design for the Sheldonian is knowable. The presence of a drawing by Hawksmoor for an independent commission, not earlier than 1716, suggests the possibility that some of the collection passed through his hands.

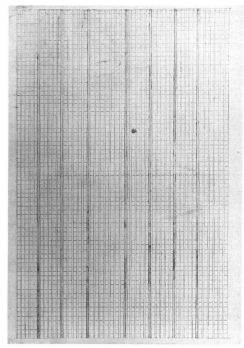

220. Unidentified

Grid Drawing

993 x 658

Pen & yellow wash

The only suggestion made for this is that it represents the bearers for the nave paving. The degree of repetition involved is exceptional.

ENGRAVINGS

The collection also includes the following engravings, which are listed here by SP numbers.

55   *West Prospect*. Schwertfäger delin. Parr. sculp.

56   *East prospect*. Schwertfäger delin. Parr sculp.

57   *South Prospect*. Schwertfäger delin. Parr sculp.

99   *West Prospect* [elevation]. Tho. Platt sculp. Upper half.

101   West front *Ex autographo architecti*. S. Gribelin 1702. Upper half.

102   Duplicate of SP 99 with dome cut away.

103   Lower half corresponding to SP 102.

104   North elevation *Ex autographo architecti*.

107   South elevation of Great Model. H. Hulsbergh.

108   Duplicate of SP 107.

109   Perspective of Great Model from south-west. J. Schynvoet.

117   West-east section of Great Model. H. Hulsbergh.

119   East-west section with dome 'according to a Former Design' (see Cat. No. 94).

The engravings SP 52, 53, 54, 76, 77, 100, 105, 106 and 110 are still at St Paul's.

INDEX

SP	Cat	SP	Cat	SP	Cat	SP	Cat	SP	Cat	Bute	Cat
1	60	39	26	85	171	127B	37	157	151	1	1
2	59	40	27	86	172	128	123	158	211	2	2
3	61	41	136	87	180	129A	31	159	212	3	3
4	54	42	127	88	182	129B	32	160	213	4	218
5	70	43	124	89	194	130	47	161	98	5	162
6	63	44	165	90	195	131	43	162	100	6	161
7	75	45	116	91	93	132	46	163	87	7	156
8	67	46	117	92A	103	133A	6	164	97	8	154
9	23	47	28	92B	126	133B	20	165A	99	9	155
10	204	48	9	93	104	134A	19	165B	92	10	73
11	106	49	205	94	210	134B	21	166	91	11	17
12	105	50	134	95	102	135	138	167	89	12	41
13	108	51	163	96	24	136A	130	168A	96	13	36
14	5	58	77	97	55	136B	119	168B	86	14	85
15	107	59	8	98	49	137	128	169A	160	15	110
16	206	60	78	111	157	138	114	169B	131	16	109
17	201	61	66	112A	88	139A	120	170	101	17	62
18	190	62	79	112B	207	139B	125	171	95	18	208
19	209	63	52	113	159	139C	121	172	90	19	166
20	71	64	30	114	48	140	132	173	214	20	167
21	68	65	74	115	51	141	133	174	215	21	169
22	64	66	58	116	57	142	219	175	216	22	175
23	65	67	4	118	94	143	135	176	217	23	176
24	69	68	45	120	76	144	16	177A	129	24	189
25	72	69	80	121A	56	145	140	177B	193	25	188
26	44	70	42	121B	7	146	142	178	183	26	173
27	10	71	81	122A	34	147	144	179	184	27	191
28	14	72	83	122B	35	148	139	180	196	28	192
29	22	73	118	123A	111	149	141	181	197	29	202
30	18	74	122	123B	112	150	153	182A	198	30	200
31	11	75	115	124	113	151A	143	182B	187	31	220
32	137	78	168	125A	82	151B	148	183	185	32	203
33	15	79	177	125B	84	152	152	184	186		
34	12	80	178	126A	38	153	150	185	199		
35	50	81	174	126B	40	154	149	186/1	158		
36	13	82	170	126C	39	155	145	186/2	164		
37	29	83	179	126D	33	156A	146				
38	25	84	181	127A	53	156B	147				